Following John

"The deceptive simplicity of the Fourth Gospel has always encouraged its readers to reflect on their way with Jesus. In *Following John*, Bill Loader presents critical scholarly insight in accessible and engaging English to support that process. His colloquial translation captures the Gospel's language while his reflections guide 'followers' toward its theological depth. He offers an excellent guide for preachers or anyone wanting a clear and focused companion to the Gospel of John."

—Harold Attridge, Sterling Professor of Divinity, emeritus, Yale University Divinity School

"With this volume, William Loader, an internationally renowned scholar, provides a delightfully insightful introduction to the Gospel of John for any reader who wants to gain a deeper appreciation of the Gospel that has shaped so much of Christian thought and devotion. Each section begins with a fresh, colloquial translation of a bite-sized chunk of the text that is followed by a brief exposition that guides readers to its major themes while anticipating and answering questions they might well raise. The book's informal style fits well with the evangelist's 'playfulness' but serious intent. Whether a first-time reader of the Gospel or one who knows it well, everyone who spends a few minutes a day with this commentary will want to return to it time and again."

—R. Alan Culpepper, McAfee School of Theology, Mercer University, Atlanta, Georgia

"William Loader's commentary provides a vital resource for readers of John who want to understand it in a relevant and timely way, without being engulfed in technicalities. With its vernacular translation, its up-to-date reflections on the text, and its questions for further reflection, this is a simple and accessible commentary. It is written by an eminent Johannine scholar who knows his material so well that he can communicate it with clarity and lucidity."

—Dorothy A. Lee, professor emerita, Trinity College, University of Divinity

"I have enjoyed reading this and have found it accessible in both language and format. I have appreciated the way that Loader can take us to the root of the passage in its original context, help us to appreciate what was meant by the author, and challenge us to look at it through the lens of a further two thousand years of thought, science, and experience. This commentary offers hope for the present and future."

—**Andrew Cunningham**, minister, Orange Uniting Church, New South Wales, Australia

"Bill Loader takes us on a journey following John. Along the way there are helpful stops to converse with Matthew, Mark, and Luke and opportunities to learn something of the Jewish and Roman culture of the time. Our guide has been exploring this road for fifty years—its promises and its puzzles. This is an invaluable resource for the preacher and pilgrim."

—**Alan Robinson**, retired minister, Uniting Church in Australia

Following John

A Commentary for People on the Road

BY
William Loader

CASCADE *Books* • Eugene, Oregon

FOLLOWING JOHN
A Commentary for People on the Road

Copyright © 2025 William Loader. All rights reserved. Except for brief quotations in critical publications or reviews, no part of this book may be reproduced in any manner without prior written permission from the publisher. Write: Permissions, Wipf and Stock Publishers, 199 W. 8th Ave., Suite 3, Eugene, OR 97401.

Cascade Books
An Imprint of Wipf and Stock Publishers
199 W. 8th Ave., Suite 3
Eugene, OR 97401

www.wipfandstock.com

PAPERBACK ISBN: 979-8-3852-3120-1
HARDCOVER ISBN: 979-8-3852-3121-8
EBOOK ISBN: 979-8-3852-3122-5

Cataloguing-in-Publication data:

Names: Loader, William R. G., 1944– [author].

Title: Following John : a commentary for people on the road / by William Loader.

Description: Eugene, OR: Cascade Books, 2025.

Identifiers: ISBN 979-8-3852-3120-1 (paperback) | ISBN 979-8-3852-3121-8 (hardcover) | ISBN 979-8-3852-3122-5 (ebook)

Subjects: LCSH: Bible.—John—Commentaries. | Commentaries.

Classification: BS2615.53 L63 2025 (paperback) | BS2615.53 (ebook)

VERSION NUMBER 03/05/25

Contents

Preface | vii

Introducing John | 1

1 **At Last, the Real Thing!** | 1
    This Is Big! (1:1–18) 5
    From John to Jesus (1:19–34) 11
    "Come and See!" (1:35–51) 15
    The Old and the New (2:1–22) 22
    Born from Above (2:23—3:36) 27
    The Water of Life (4:1–54) 35

2 **Claims Contested** | 41
    Resurrection Now (5:1–47) 41
    The Bread of Life (6:1–71) 47
    Who Is This Fellow? (7:1—8:11) 56
    The Devil's Children! (8:12–59) 63
    Who's Really Blind? (9:1–41) 68

3 **Facing Rejection** | 73
    The Good Shepherd and His Sheep (10:1–42) 73
    The Resurrection and the Life (11:1–57) 79
    Facing the End (12:1–50) 85

4 Famous Last Words | 93

Love—All the Way (13:1–38) 93

Don't Let Yourselves Get Stressed and Anxious! (14:1–31) 102

Love and Hate (15:1–27) 109

Hope and New Beginnings (16:1–33) 113

Praying for Them and for Us (17:1–26) 118

5 The End and the Beginning | 123

Betrayal, Arrest, and Denial (18:1–27) 123

Jesus Before Pilate (18:28—19:16) 129

Execution and Entombment (19:16–42) 136

Easter and Pentecost All in One (20:1–31) 142

Where to from Here? (21:1–25) 149

Concluding Reflection | 155

Preface

PEOPLE IN MINISTRY TODAY face increasing pressures, leaving them often with little time to consult good commentaries in preparation for preaching. Part of my response to this has been to offer brief commentaries on the texts from the New Testament set in the Lectionary from Sunday to Sunday. I am aware that thousands worldwide make use of these resources freely available on my website (billloader.com). At the same time, it has struck me that it is also useful to see texts in their context and so to read them within their narrative frame, in other words, to hear the whole story as the Gospel writers tell it.

I have also become aware that increasingly church members have been wanting a more informed faith. That includes not just reading and hearing biblical texts but understanding them in the light of the culture of their day, informed by up-to-date scholarship. The aim of this series is also to address that need and so provide a resource for individuals and groups wanting more substance and depth. To aid this I have added after each section a reflective comment, but in addition the resources work best when people simply identify what it was that was new or especially interesting in what they have read. The aim is to promote an open engagement, including critical engagement, with the text that acknowledges questions, explores background, and confronts what we can and cannot know of its meaning.

I have taken units of text, sometimes following chapter divisions, sometimes following sense divisions, and offered a translation under the heading of *Listening to John* followed by commentary under the heading, *Thinking About John*. In the translation I have sought to stay close to the Greek text but to express the translation in less formal English than is usually the case, which may include, from time to time, Australian idioms whose meaning will nevertheless be obvious. Apart from when I cite John and Mark, all other quotations use the NRSV translation.

The Fourth Gospel is a special text which has enriched faith down through the centuries through its method of taking up traditions like those found in the other Gospels and then creatively enhancing them to produce an image of Jesus that has been able to be appreciated across many cultures, not least through its use of imagery central to human existence, such as water, bread, light, and life. I have sought to provide an up-to-date, concise, informed, and readable commentary that will help people find enrichment in engaging this wonderful Gospel.

At a personal level this Gospel has been one of the foci of my academic research over the past fifty years. Some of that research is represented in my books, *Christology, Soteriology, and Ethics in John and Hebrews: Collected Essays* (Tübingen: Mohr Siebeck, 2022); *Jesus in John's Gospel: Structure and Issues in Johannine Christology* (Grand Rapids: Eerdmans, 2017), and *Jesus' Attitude Towards the Law: A Study of the Gospels* (Tübingen: Mohr Siebeck, 1997; Grand Rapids: Eerdmans, 2002). In undertaking such research, I have benefited so much by engagement with other scholars in the field. I am also now deeply grateful to Revd Alan and Sharyn Robinson, and my wife Gisela, for careful reading.

William Loader

Introducing John

THE GOSPEL ACCORDING TO John sits alongside the Gospels according to Matthew, Mark, and Luke, but has a character all of its own. The first three Gospels are closely connected. On the most widely accepted reconstruction of the relationship, Mark wrote his Gospel first, around 70 CE, and the other two used and revised Mark and supplemented it independently of each other. They were able to use some extra material to which they both had access, which mainly comprised sayings of Jesus, but also to use sources to which each had sole access. They were most likely writing around fifteen years after Mark. When we study those Gospels closely, we can see how they revised Mark, rearranged material, corrected or enhanced it, and generally adapted it to serve what they wanted to emphasize about Jesus.

When we come to the Gospel according to John, we are immediately confronted with a problem. The language the author has Jesus use, the way he talks in the many dialogues and speeches it contains, is different from what we find in the other Gospels. It doubtless reflects the way that the author and the circles to which he belonged had come to think and speak about Jesus. In part this reflects best practice at the time among authors who undertook to write biographies of famous people of the past. That included seeking to have those historical figures speak to the contemporary contexts in which the biographers wrote in terms that their audiences would relate to. Luke does this when he writes Acts, creating speeches for the key figures, but in his Gospel he sticks with the short anecdotes that had formed part of the tradition.

The author of John's Gospel has as his sole focus the goal of presenting Jesus as the Son of God come from heaven to offer eternal life on God's behalf. This is the golden thread that runs through the entire Gospel. Much in the speeches and dialogues is about making the claim that this is who he is. He is God's agent and offers what God offers, expressed in almost endless variation, including through the use of imagery like water, bread, light, and life. The focus is all on having eternal life with God through Jesus and ultimately joining him in the heavenly world. In contrast, the Jesus of the first three Gospels focuses on the kingdom of God, meaning God's coming reign, which would bring change and hope to a needy world and was already breaking into reality through Jesus' ministry.

The author of John's Gospel is also talking about this same Jesus. He clearly knows many of the stories and anecdotes we find in Mark, so that most scholars these days assume that he had some familiarity with Mark and perhaps also with, at least, Luke as well, but not in the same way as Matthew and Luke, who obviously had Mark in front of them. Rather, our Gospel author knew the substance of much of what is in Mark, including the occasional tell-tale details confirming this, but it was a distant familiarity. He used such stories as a launching pad for his own elaborate claims. A good example is his use of the story of Jesus feeding five thousand people found in Mark. Our author uses it as the basis for a lengthy dialogue and speech in which Jesus claims to be the bread of life.

We have, therefore, in John's Gospel both extensive elaboration as well as older tradition. Some of that older tradition may well preserve detail that reaches right back in history to the days of the historical Jesus and is immensely valuable. Some detail leaves us pondering whether it reflects better history than the others or just the author's creative elaboration. For instance, was the Friday on which Jesus died Passover Day, as the first three Gospels portray it, or was it the day before Passover Day, as John reports? Similarly, did Jesus' ministry from his baptism to his death last one year, as the first three portray it, or three years, as John's Gospel portrays it?

Like the other Gospels, the Gospel According to John, does not identify its author. At most, it hints that it has a connection with a mysterious unnamed favorite disciple of Jesus, who, it claims, lies behind its portrait. Second-century guesses conjectured by elimination that this must have been one of Jesus' twelve disciples, namely, John, one of the sons of Zebedee, whose brother was executed in 44 CE, and concluded that John must be the author. Hence, the designation of the Gospel as John's.

To avoid endless repetition of phrases like the author of John's Gospel, I shall from this point on write of the author as John, although I consider it highly unlikely that the author was the disciple John. It would be extraordinary that he would have heard so much that the other Gospels did not and have had such a different picture of Jesus. They, too, do not identify their author, and their names are similarly largely guesswork, or, at most, reflect the likelihood that they were composed in settings that in some way had been influenced by the figures so named.

Little is to be gained by speculation about who the real authors might have been. On the other hand, we can already know so much about them, or at least about what mattered to them, by what and how they wrote. It makes little sense to imagine that they began writing their Gospels from scratch, even making it up as they went along. Rather, we need to recognize that they will have been telling and retelling stories about Jesus within communities of faith and have been doing it regularly before putting it all in writing. In John's Gospel we may well see signs of this in his elaboration of the story of the feeding of the five thousand, for instance, where some see traces of earlier versions still visible in the final form.

The same is very much true of the five-chapter-long account of Jesus' final words to his disciples in John 13–17. The speech seems to end in John 14 when Jesus tells them to get up and go and so John 18 seems to report what happened next, but the final version has another three chapters in between. Composing farewell speeches of famous people was common. It was an attempt to bring home their significance for future generations. It was standard practice. Mark has Jesus' final speech in Mark 13, which includes what he portrays as Jesus' advice about the destruction of the temple in 70 CE, an event that must have happened shortly before Mark wrote. Matthew expands the speech from one chapter to two (Matthew 24–25), and Luke, like John, relocates the final speech to the setting of Jesus' last meal (Luke 22:24–38) and takes up material that Mark had placed earlier and uses it for the purpose.

We suspect that John must have been written some time in the 90s CE, well after Mark but also after Matthew and Luke. It will have been written in the context of faith communities who had developed distinctive ways of talking about Jesus. There are signs throughout that at least in their history they had been engaged in dispute with other Jews and some of this would have meant conflict and debate between Jews who embraced the message of Jesus as portrayed by John and those who did not.

What Jews had claimed of the Law, as God's gift and God's Word brought to them by God's Wisdom, often personified as Lady Wisdom, these followers of Jesus were now claiming of Jesus. *He* was God's Wisdom, God's Word, become flesh in the person of Jesus, and so they transferred imagery used of the Law to Jesus, such as water of life, bread of life, light, and life.

They went further and claimed that he was exclusively so and that this had been God's plan, set out, as they claimed, in the Law itself. These tensions are frequently a backdrop for the dialogues, indeed disputes, and speeches in the Gospel. They also seem to reflect the pain and anger felt by the Jesus-following Jewish communities whose own experiences of rejection by fellow Jews are reflected in this telling of the story of Jesus.

John also appears to have had access to what was probably a collection of miracles of Jesus which in some circles must have been used primarily for propaganda purpose, that is, in evangelism, to persuade people to believe. Many are quite fantastic and similar to the magic attributed to other people of fame and claimed by emperors in their political propaganda about themselves. Jesus could turn water into wine, heal from a great distance, bring the dead back to life, as well as multiply food and walk on water, as Mark already reported. We should not imagine that John would doubt such stories, but it is clear that part of his agenda in writing is to direct attention away from the "wow" effect to what he saw as the true *meaning* of the miracles. They are to be seen as evidence of who Jesus was, and frequently as symbolically representing that, as giver of the bread of life and as the source of resurrection in a deeper sense.

The author, therefore, draws on sources that he will have found in use in faith communities in his world, such as, at least, Mark, but also collections of wonders. Using the rhetorical skills he will have learned through the education processes of his time, he creates an account of who Jesus was that is rich in meaning. By employing imagery related to basic human need worldwide, such as thirst for water, hunger for bread, light, and life, he has presented a Jesus who addresses universal human need. His is arguably, therefore, the Gospel with widest appeal.

The focus is Jesus, but ultimately the God whom he represents. This Gospel produced a version of the Christian gospel that put the emphasis on finding life in a relationship with God, indeed with God as one who loves. Another from the same circle, the author of 1 John, would some years later simply declare, "God is love," in appealing to people in his faith communities, therefore, to show love and care for one another.

Reading John's Gospel is like listening to a symphony or at least to a symphonic movement, where a central melody sounds across the whole piece, played by clarinet or flute or violin or double base. Variations on a theme, to be listened to and enjoyed. It is the theme of the Son come from above, sent by the Father with the offer of life.

1

At Last, the Real Thing!

This Is Big! (John 1:1–18)

Listening to John

¹:¹ In the beginning was the Word and the Word was with God and the Word was God. ² He was in the beginning with God. ³ Everything came into existence through him and not a single thing came into existence independent of him. What came into being ⁴ through him was life and that life was the light for human beings. ⁵ And the light shines in the darkness and the darkness has not snuffed it out.

⁶ There was a man sent from God whose name was John. ⁷ He came for the purpose of bearing witness, to bear witness to the light, so that everyone might come to faith through him. ⁸ He was not that light but came to bear witness to the light.

⁹ The true light which gives light to every person was coming into the world. ¹⁰ He was in the world and the world came into existence through him, but the world did not recognize him. ¹¹ He came to his own, and his own people did not accept him, ¹² but whoever did accept him, he gave them the right to become God's children, to those who believed in his name. ¹³ They were born not of blood, nor of the will of the flesh, nor of the will of a male, but of God.

¹⁴ And the Word became flesh and dwelt among us, and we saw his glory, the glory of the only Son of the Father, full of grace and truth. ¹⁵ John testifies about him and has made the acclamation, "This was the one of whom I spoke, the one coming after me who came into

existence before my time and was my superior." **16** For from his fullness we have all benefitted, one gift of grace in place of another gift of grace, **17** because the Law was given through Moses and grace and truth came into being through Jesus Christ. **18** God no one has ever seen, but God, the unique Son, who is in God's heart, he has opened him up to us.

Thinking About John

This is big! It is not just the story of Jesus of Nazareth acclaimed as Messiah. It is the story of the universe and its beginnings. Echoing the first words of sacred Scripture it declares that in the beginning was the Word. "The Word" translates a Greek word *logos*, behind our word logic, and was used in one stream of Greek philosophy to describe the substance which penetrates the universe and holds it all together, its logic, its meaning and reason (which are also ways of translating the word *logos*).

John's Gospel is about the meaning of the universe in that sense. It is also written from a Jewish perspective, familiar not only with the terms of Greek science but also with its own rich tradition, which spoke of God's Wisdom active in creation, and sometimes it merged the two concepts of Word and Wisdom together. The meaning of the universe is to be found in divine Wisdom, sometimes pictured as God's intimate female companion and friend. Such images slide into the language of myth, which can then speak of Wisdom, Sophia, as like the highest angel and as bearing God's image, reflecting his glory. Some went even further to equate God's Wisdom and Word with God's Law given in Scripture, the basis, like the Greek *logos*, of order and meaning in the universe.

Such reflections inspire the Gospel's introduction, taking its readers back to when the universe came into being, by their reckoning, based on biblical genealogies and reference to ages, around four thousand years before their time. This is a long way short of the 13.7 billion years that modern science reckons, and it reflects an earth-centered view of the universe and an understanding of earth as flat (or, at most, spherical but with the sun circling it—if such early Greek theories had entered their world). Despite these differences concerning both time and space, the Gospel asserts that the story it wants to tell is ultimately about the meaning of the universe, the meaning of life.

The combination of asserting this fundamental claim and couching it in language and imagery belonging to earlier speculation creates some apparently contradictory statements. How, for instance, can the Word be *with* God and *be* God at the same time? In what sense are the Word and God distinct, and in what sense are they one? The matter becomes all the more complicated when the author clearly wants to identify Jesus as the Word and goes on in the narrative to have Jesus obey God and pray to God.

Some of these issues go back to the way Jewish tradition portrayed God's Wisdom as in some way existing alongside God. Proverbs depicts Wisdom as saying:

> The LORD created me at the beginning of his work, the first of his acts of long ago. [23] Ages ago I was set up, at the first, before the beginning of the earth. (Prov 8:22–23)

and goes on to speak of Wisdom as God's companion:

> then I was beside him, like a master worker; and I was daily his delight, rejoicing before him always. (Prov 8:30)

The writing Ben Sira, preserved in the Apocrypha, speaks of Wisdom seeking for a place to dwell and reports:

> Then the Creator of all things gave me a command, and my Creator chose the place for my tent. He said, "Make your dwelling in Jacob, and in Israel receive your inheritance." (Sir 24:8)

and goes on to say:

> All this is the book of the covenant of the Most High God, the Law that Moses commanded us as an inheritance for the congregations of Jacob. (Sir 24:24)

Luke even brings a saying of Jesus that speaks about Wisdom:

> Therefore also the Wisdom of God said, "I will send them prophets and apostles, some of whom they will kill and persecute." (Luke 11:49)

Such flexibility of thought made it possible to speak of Wisdom/Word as God and at the same time as God's agent, as a separate being, and even as God's commands, as in the Law. If Wisdom could manifest itself through Moses and the prophets, it was not such a radical step to declare that Wisdom manifested itself in Jesus and that Jesus is the Word.

There are tensions and loose ends in such language, and it resulted in centuries of theory trying to fit it all together. The author makes no attempt to do so, but simply asserts that the story of Jesus begins as the story of Wisdom, the Word, who was with God and was God, and so makes God known and reveals the meaning of existence.

The second verse emphasizes the point: he was with God in the beginning. What then follows is a standard description of the role of Wisdom/Word in creating and sustaining all things and bringing life. This is more than simple existence. Ultimately it is the life that comes from God and so can also serve as a description of what, according to the Gospel, was the life that Jesus offered. His story, yet to be told, is already represented in the comment that the light shines and darkness cannot stop it, like a hint of crucifixion and resurrection right from the opening words.

Jesus' actual story begins as it did in our earliest gospel, Mark: with John the Baptist (John 1:6–8). There was no explaining away that link; it was too deeply rooted in tradition and history, awkward as it was sometimes found to be. The author's take on the problem was to allow that John was a witness to who Jesus was, but no more. Later in the chapter he spells that out in detail. John bore witness to the light that was to offer light to all coming into the world.

That event, his entry into the world, met with both rejection and acceptance (1:10–11). It sounds initially like no one accepted him, but then we hear that some did. Jewish tradition reflected in the Parables of Enoch, a writing also from the same century, also knew an account of Wisdom coming to God's people only to be rebuffed (1 En. 42). Coming to his own is probably a reference here in John 1:11 to his own Jewish people, rather than to all created beings. Those who did accept him then qualified to be called God's children, whether they had been Jews or not (1:12). This is a switch of values that implicitly denies that his own Jewish people could any longer claim to be God's children and reflects sharp division within Jewish communities. Becoming God's children is not a matter of race. The image of a new birth, a new beginning, will return when the author has Jesus confront the inadequate faith of Nicodemus (3:3).

The author has twice already referred to Jesus' coming as the Word (1:9, 11). He comes at it a third time in 1:14 with more specific detail: "The Word became flesh and dwelt among us." The flexibility of language means that the Word did not cease to exist and instead became flesh but became embodied as the human being Jesus. Later, we will see that some were inclined to see Jesus therefore not as a real human being but merely as a divine being in disguise.

Saying he became flesh is striking and serves in part to ward off any watering down of Jesus' humanity. It did however create more problems for later generations who had to develop explanations for how Jesus could be both the divine Word and a genuine human being. Did he, for instance, have superhuman knowledge and powers? What about the limitations of the human brain and memory? Did he have two brains or two souls? How could he be both? The author offers no explanations and employs his language with a flexibility that defies precision.

He is not wanting to propound a complex doctrine of the person of Christ. He is using the Wisdom/Word mythology to uphold the claim that in Jesus people encountered the offer of life with God in a unique way. Matthew and Luke explained how it could be by attributing it in part to his miraculous conception. John attributes it to his oneness with the Word, his identity as the Word, while paradoxically remaining fully human, a seeming impossibility left unexplained, but asserting what for the author and his listeners was central to their faith.

That faith claimed, as the author goes on to say, that in him they saw someone who was indeed at the same time God's Son, full of grace and truth. Grace, generous accepting love, was really what mattered and his status as its bearer set him above both John the Baptist and the Law that God gave to Moses, because, for the author, the role of both was to point to this gift in place of all previous gifts, including that gift of the Law.

The author's claim is that, in contrast to all who had gone before, none of whom had seen God, Jesus as the Word had known and seen God (1:18) and so was therefore uniquely qualified to make God known. Making God known was not to offer information, but to offer a relationship, to offer God's grace, God's generous accepting love. These are big claims and are the basis for all that follows. Time and time again the author presents Jesus as the one who makes God known, frequently using the image of Jesus as an envoy sent to make God known, but always what the envoy brings is not information but an invitation to relationship. This is the golden thread that we find through John's Gospel.

These opening verses function as an introduction, setting the scene for what follows, an overture that reflects the main melodies that follow. It has an artistic quality, which has suggested to some that the author is making use of pre-existing poetic material. It may have once depicted Wisdom/

Word as coming first in prophets and sages and then only in 1:14 moving on to speak of coming in Jesus, and some still see it that way. It certainly has a different, more artistic feel about it than the rest of the Gospel, where we do not again hear in the same style of Jesus as the Word. The author has probably deliberately chosen the universal perspective that it offers in order to alert his hearers to the broader significance of what follows. It is the key to unlocking what he was wanting to say throughout, as he takes up traditional anecdotes and sayings of Jesus and imaginatively portrays him as elucidating the claims being made in this impressive preface.

Reflection: What makes John's Gospel universal in its appeal?

From John to Jesus (John 1:19–34)

Listening to John

^{1:19} And this is the testimony of John, when the Jews sent priests and Levites from Jerusalem to ask him, "Who are you?"

²⁰ He confessed and did not deny, but confessed, "I am not the Messiah."

²¹ And they asked him, "What then? Are you Elijah?"

And he said, "I'm not."

"Are you the prophet?"

He replied, "No."

²² So they said to him, "Who are you? Tell us, so we can give an answer to those who sent us. What do you say about yourself?"

He said, ²³ "I am a voice calling in the outback, 'Make a straight road for the Lord,' like Isaiah the prophet said."

²⁴ And they had been sent from the Pharisees ²⁵ and questioned him, saying, "Why are you baptizing if you are not the Messiah, nor Elijah, nor the prophet?"

²⁶ John responded, "I baptize in water. In your midst someone is standing who you don't know about. ²⁷ He is the one coming after me, whose sandal straps I'm not worthy to untie."

²⁸ These things took place in Bethany on the other side of the Jordan river where John was baptizing. ²⁹ The next day he saw Jesus approaching him and said, "Look, the lamb of God who takes the sin of the world away. ³⁰ This is the one of whom I spoke, a man is coming after me, who came into existence before me, because he was my superior. ³¹ And I did not recognize him. But to reveal him to Israel, that is why I came baptizing in water."

³² And John testified, saying, "I saw the Spirit coming down like a dove from heaven and coming to rest on him. ³³ I did not recognize him, but the one who sent me to baptize in water, he told me, 'The person on whom you see the Spirit come down and rest, this is the

one who baptizes with the Holy Spirit.' ³⁴ And I have seen and have witnessed that this man is the Son of God."

Thinking About John

From the heights of careful artistic expression found in the opening verses, 1:1–18, the author takes us, in what follows, into storytelling. Already in the introduction he had signaled a concern to differentiate Jesus from John the Baptist with comments that seem to intrude into its poetry (1:6–8, 15). John was not the light of the world, although as the author later reveals, there were claims that spoke of him as a shining light. This is reflected in words the author attributes to Jesus, himself: "He was a burning and shining lamp, and you were willing to rejoice for a while in his light" (5:35), when he was about to claim that he was greater than John (5:36).

Much of chapter 1 is taken up with recalibrating John's significance. It is highly likely that one of the reasons for doing so was that there was a movement that continued to hail John and had become a rival or at least in some sense a competitor to the Jesus movement in the author's world. That movement continued and survives to the present day, especially in what came to be called the Mandaean religious movement. The effort to put John in his place is strident, the author almost bending over backwards to emphasize the difference as in his introduction to John's reply to priests and Levites sent from Jerusalem: "He confessed and did not deny but confessed" (1:20)!

The author was engaged in a careful balancing act. There was no way he could badmouth John. John had, after all, baptized Jesus, and the memory was too strong that Jesus started with John. He has, however, to put John in his place and so has him deny not only that he was the Messiah but also that he was Elijah, as Mark's Jesus suggested (Mark 9:11–13), or the prophet like Moses (1:20–21). Only after such denials does the author bring the tradition found in the other Gospels of portraying John as the voice crying out in the outback (1:23; Mark 1:3; Matt 3:3; Luke 3:4).

In reworking the traditions found in the other Gospels about John the Baptist, the author has removed any mention of John's baptism having to do with forgiveness of sins, because, for the author, forgiveness comes only through Jesus. He takes up the saying attributed to John about one coming after him whose sandals he would be unworthy to untie (Mark 1:7) but extends and explains it. Already in 1:15 the author had reported: "John testified to him and cried out, 'This was he of whom I said, "He who comes after me ranks ahead of me because he was before me."'" In this way he alludes to Jesus as being the Word who was with God in the beginning, so very much "before" him in time. The author repeats John's statement about his inferiority twice more (1:27, 30), again on the second occasion pointing to Jesus' having been in existence before him.

The rewriting of the account of Jesus' baptism by John, a core element not to be explained away, indicates that the descent of the Spirit as a dove was not to enter Jesus but to alight on him and then remain on him, meant not literally, but symbolically, to emphasize Jesus' permanent full connection with the Spirit, a claim later alluded to in 3:34 ("he doesn't just have the Spirit in a partial way"). This also avoids a reading that would suggest that this was the moment when Jesus received the Spirit, as if he did not always have it. The author also repurposes it to suggest it was also the God-given signal to John the Baptist that Jesus was the one to come of whom he had spoken. The author twice has John repeat that he would not otherwise have known who Jesus was (1:31, 33). He then has John declare Jesus to be Son of God. This, too, is a reworking of tradition. For, according to tradition, it was the divine voice from heaven that addressed Jesus as God's Son, as in Mark, "You are my Son," addressed to Jesus (Mark 1:11), and in Matthew re-addressed to all: "This my Son" (Matt 3:17).

The author has thus redefined John's role to make him not a prophet preparing the way by a baptism for forgiveness of sins but a witness who points to who Jesus is, as he puts it, "to reveal him to Israel" (1:31).

The author retains one of the other key elements first found in Mark, namely that Jesus' role is to baptize with the Spirit: "this is the one who baptizes with the Holy Spirit" (1:33). Our church calendar year leads us to see in this a reference to the Day of Pentecost in Acts 2, following Luke's interpretation, but already in Mark it refers not to that event but to the activities in which Jesus was about to engage. Mark has Jesus warn that not to recognize the work of the Spirit in his ministry is unforgiveable blasphemy (Mark 3:28–29). Neither Mark nor John uses the language of baptizing with the Spirit in their accounts of Jesus' ministry, but, like Mark, John's Gospel certainly assumes it refers to Jesus' ministry, and has this echoed in his final address to his disciples. For in speaking of the Spirit he refers to its presence with the disciples while he was with them and the time to come when the Spirit would take up residence in them: "because it remains with you and will be in you" (14:17).

The next serious reworking of earlier tradition about John comes in the dramatic declaration: "Look, the lamb of God who takes away the sin of the world!" (1:29). Thus, no longer seen by the author as offering a baptism for the forgiveness of sins, he makes it thereby very clear: Jesus and Jesus alone is the one who will take sin away.

Many see in the depiction of Jesus as a lamb a reflection of the well-entrenched interpretation of Jesus' death as a sacrifice. That is certainly possible, but an alternative or an additional interpretation is to see it as an allusion to what he would do in his ministry, namely, offering eternal life, which always included forgiveness of sin. A lamb, and sometimes a ram, was an image for the Jewish Messiah. The following context makes it very clear how the disciples who heard John declare Jesus to be the lamb understood it. They heard John telling them that Jesus was the Messiah and so that is what they go on to tell others. Messiahship was also the theme at the beginning of this section where John must make it clear that he is not the Messiah and it is how the section ends with Nathanael declaring that Jesus is the Son of God (as John had heard) and the King of Israel, also titles used of the expected Messiah figure. To add to the richness of the imagery, the word for "lamb" in Aramaic can also mean servant and so allude to Jesus as God's servant, the Messiah.

There is a sense in which the author continues putting John in his place when he depicts two of John's disciples hearing John repeat his declaration, "Look, the lamb of God!" (1:36), and then leaving him to follow Jesus (1:37). The implication: all John's disciples should do the same!

Reflection: The author has shaped this section of the story in the light of how he has presented Jesus as the Word: Where do you see this happening?

"Come and See!" (John 1:35–51)

Listening to John

1:35 The next day John was again standing there with two of his disciples, **36** and seeing Jesus walking along he said, "Look, the lamb of God!" **37** And his two disciples heard what he was saying and followed Jesus. **38** Jesus turned round and saw them following him and said to them, "What are you looking for?"

They said to him, "Rabbi (which translated means teacher), where are you staying?"

39 He said to them, "Come and you'll see!"

So they came and saw where he was staying and hung out with him there that day. It was about four in the afternoon. **40** Andrew, the brother of Simon Peter, was one of the two disciples who had heard John and followed him. **41** He first found his own brother, Simon, and told him, "We've found the Messiah" (which translated is anointed one). **42** And he brought him to Jesus.

Looking at him Jesus said, "You are Simon son of John; you will be called Cephas" (which translated means Peter).

43 The next day he decided to leave for Galilee and found Philip. And Jesus said to him, "Follow me!" **44** Philip was from Bethsaida, from Andrew and Peter's town. **45** Philip found Nathanael and told him, "We've found the one Moses in the Law and the prophets wrote about, namely, Jesus from Nazareth, Joseph's son."

46 And Nathanael replied to him, "Can anything good come out of Nazareth?"

And Philip said to him, "Come and see!"

47 Jesus saw Nathanael coming to him and said of him, "Look, here's a true Israelite, nothing false about him!"

48 Nathanael said to him, "How come you know about me?"

Jesus replied, telling him, "Before Philip called you, when you were under the fig tree, I saw you."

⁴⁹ Nathanael responded, "Rabbi, you are the Son of God, you are the King of Israel!"

⁵⁰ Jesus answered, "Because I told you I saw you under the fig tree you believe? You will see greater things than these." ⁵¹ And he told him, "Truly, truly I tell you, you will see the heaven opened and angels of God ascending and descending upon the Son of Man."

Thinking About John

While, like the other Gospels, this one follows the account of John the Baptist with stories about Jesus calling his first disciples, building his team, the stories are very different. Instead of telling how Jesus called Simon Peter and Andrew his brother while they were fishing in Lake Galilee (Mark 1:15–18), the Fourth Gospel has Andrew named as one of the two disciples of John the Baptist, who left and followed Jesus. Then the author has Andrew, not Jesus, go and find Peter, his brother, and tell him he had found the Messiah and bring him to Jesus.

This incident, hailed as a model of evangelism and sometimes called "Operation Andrew," may well reflect another agenda, namely a tendency of the author to acknowledge Peter's leadership but slightly demote him in favor of the tradition his Gospel represents. This subtle twist may well reflect tensions between the circle of churches to which this Gospel belongs with others who claimed Peter's authority.

It looks like a creative reworking of the stories that were circulating about Peter, which included that Jesus named him Cephas, the Aramaic word for rock, which was then translated into Greek as *petros* and comes through into English as Peter. Matthew's Gospel plays with the word to have Jesus declare Peter the foundation rock of the church (16:18). In a sense, if his was the first encounter with the risen Jesus, as Mark and others suggest (16:7; 1 Cor 15:5; Luke 24:34), then this was true.

John also knows of the miraculous catch of fish that Jesus initiated when he told Peter to cast his net on the other side of his boat, a story told in Luke's account of Peter's initial call (Luke 5:1–11), but John brings it only after his account of Jesus' resurrection, when Jesus encounters a group of his disciples along with Peter in Galilee (John 21:1–11).

Perhaps the story did owe its origin to such Easter stories. Sometimes the author appears to bring information that indicates that his sources contained accurate data, especially about names and places. Was Bethsaida Peter and Andrew's hometown, as he reports? According to John, it was also Philip's (12:21), of whom we hear almost nothing in the other Gospels. It is sometimes very difficult to know what is creative rewriting and what is history.

The exchange that John then brings between Philip and Nathanael and then Nathanael and Jesus is rich in meaning. First, Jesus calls Philip and then Philip finds Nathanael and declares: "We have found him about whom Moses in the Law and also the prophets wrote, Jesus from Nazareth, Joseph's son" (1:45). Nathanael's reply, "Can anything good come out of Nazareth?" may indicate that people from Bethsaida held prejudice towards the people of Nazareth or perhaps the author wants us to see Jesus as typically facing an uphill climb against prejudice.

Like Andrew, Philip's focus is on Jesus as the promised Messiah, the Christ. It was already the topic in exchanges with John the Baptist who vehemently denied that he was the Messiah and may, as noted above, also be reflected in the reference to Jesus as the lamb. Nathanael will go on to hail Jesus with two of the titles associated with Messiah: "Son of God" (adopted as God's vice regent on earth) and "King of Israel."

Hope for such a Messiah was potentially explosive because usually it expressed the hope that God would raise up a hero like King David to liberate the land from its ills and usually also to drive out the Romans, a claim sure to have you end up being crucified. While clearly not seeing Jesus as militant and so finding no need to arrest his disciples along with him, Pilate did see Jesus and his proclamation of good news for the poor and hungry in God's coming reign as calling Rome's reign into question. Such aspirations were destabilizing and would-be Messiahs, whether acclaimed by others or self-promoting, were to be firmly quashed. Jesus' resurrection revived hopes in some quarters of Jesus' return as the one appointed to fulfill that hope.

The author of John's Gospel offers no explanation of his take on the title, but it becomes clear that his is a quite different understanding, for he depicts Jesus not as a warrior figure and also not as the one to come in the kingdom, which would be good news for the poor, but as the embodiment of God's Wisdom and Word who, already in his ministry, has come to offer life. This is the golden thread running through John's Gospel. Thus, where the title is used by John of Jesus, it needs to be seen in that light. He is "Son of God," according to John, in a much deeper sense. He is the Word, the Son, come from the Father, sent to engage people in a relationship with God. He is promoting not the overthrow of the Romans; he was promoting himself as light and life and, through himself, ultimately promoting God.

The author's subtlety continues in the imagery of Nathanael sitting under the fig tree, a traditional symbol of a true and faithful Jew, seen by Jesus through supernatural power and declared by him to be an authentic representative of Israel. John assumes such miraculous powers and often depicts Jesus as performing extraordinary feats. It will not be too long into his narrative before he engages us in reflection on just what weight to give such detail. He does so in 2:23–25.

Of much greater significance is the declaration of Nathanael, who is depicted as highly qualified. Addressing Jesus as a teacher, "Rabbi," he, too, affirms Jesus' messiahship: "Rabbi, you are the Son of God! You are the King of Israel!" (1:49). Might the author have intended that we hear in this an echo of what will befall Jesus, mockingly acclaimed "King of the Jews" by Pilate?

We might have expected that Nathanael's acclamation would be the fitting climax to this opening chapter, but that is not the case. The author has Jesus himself take the lead in saying there is more to come:

> "Do you believe because I told you that I saw you under the fig tree? You will see greater things than these." And he said to him, "Very truly, I tell you, you will see heaven opened and the angels of God ascending and descending upon the Son of Man." (1:50–51)

Might the "greater things" refer to what the Gospel writer would go on to report and so have us see the following chapters as somehow represented in angels ascending and descending on the Son of Man? So even more fantastic miracles than being able to see Nathanael under the fig tree? This is much less likely than that the author has something else in mind, namely that one day Jesus would be in an exalted state adored by angels.

The imagery of angels ascending and descending is a deliberate echo of Jacob's dream where he "dreamed that there was a ladder set up on the earth, the top of it reaching to heaven; and the angels of God were ascending and descending on it" (Gen 28:12). John has changed the image somewhat so that now the angels are ascending and descending not on a ladder but on Jesus himself. It is an image of adoration. The echo, however, relates not just to the angels, but to Jacob himself, also called Israel. The new genuine

Israelite, Nathanael, is to be the one seeing Jesus' exaltation, along with others, because the author writes of "you" in the plural.

If chapter 1 began with Jesus as the Word in the beginning, it concludes with where, according to the author, Jesus is now, sharing in the glory and wonder of God as the climax of his journey of becoming flesh, being crucified, then being raised and exalted, back into God's presence. It was the author's way of explaining Jesus' significance as the one who brings us into encounter with God. He thus couches it in a story that has Jesus emerge from God's very heart and return there. As he puts it in 1:18, "God no one has ever seen, but God, the unique Son, who is in God's heart, he has opened him up to us."

The pattern of portraying the climax of Jesus' life by speaking of him as Son of Man and picturing him as now in an exalted state recurs at a number of points through John's Gospel. The preference to refer to Jesus in this context as Son of Man reflects the tradition according to which the one to hold judgment at the climax of history was sometimes pictured as God's human agent, traditionally the Son of Man, sometimes, as in John, associated also with the image of the Messiah. We see this image of Son of Man as judge mentioned in 5:27 where Jesus speaks of himself as the Son of Man: God "has authorized him to conduct judgment because he is the Son of Man."

The author frequently talks about Jesus as Son of Man or has Jesus refer to himself as Son of Man when speaking of the events that would immediately follow his death. Thus in 3:13 he has Jesus, after referring to what he was offering during his ministry, say:

> If I have told you about earthly things and you do not believe, how can you believe if I tell you about heavenly things? No one has ascended into heaven except the one who descended from heaven, the Son of Man. And just as Moses lifted up the serpent in the outback, so must the Son of Man be lifted up, that whoever believes in him may have eternal life. (3:12–14)

When Jesus speaks of himself ascending to God after his death, he uses the title Son of Man: "Then what if you were to see the Son of Man ascending to where he was before?" (6:62).

Elsewhere he depicts this not just as his return, but as bringing about significant change.

> When you have lifted up the Son of Man, then you will realize that I am he, and that I do nothing on my own, but I speak these things as the Father instructed me. (8:28)

It points to a change in understanding that will occur. That change will bring realization of who Jesus is and inaugurate mission.

> The hour has come for the Son of Man to be glorified. Very truly, I tell you, unless a grain of wheat falls into the earth and dies, it remains just a single grain; but if it dies, it bears much fruit. (12:23–24)

> And I, when I am lifted up from the earth, will draw all people to myself. He said this to indicate the kind of death he was to die. The crowd answered him, "We have heard from the law that the Messiah remains forever. How can you say that the Son of Man must be lifted up? Who is this Son of Man?" (12:32–34)

In his extensive instructions to his disciples on the night of his arrest Jesus explains that his going away will result in the sending of the Spirit, who will bring to light who Jesus was and inspire the disciples to mission.

Thus, the author frequently has Jesus refer to his ascent to the Father using the designation Son of Man and terms such as being lifted up and glorified. Thereby there is a subtle play in using the word "lifted up" because at an earthly level it refers to his execution up on a cross, but to the eyes of faith, it refers to his being lifted up to God.

At the end of his introductory section, therefore, the author points us to this climax of Jesus' life, to what at one level is a shameful end on a cross, but, in reality, is his exaltation to God's right hand with angels serving him. It is even more than that because the author also thereby points to what he will have Jesus explain in his final words:

> Very truly, I tell you, the one who believes in me will also do the works that I do and, in fact, will do greater works than these, because I am going to the Father. (14:12)

> Nevertheless, I tell you the truth: it is to your advantage that I go away, for if I do not go away, the Advocate will not come to you; but if I go, I will send him to you. (16:7)

There is a sense in which John 1 brings what is essential for understanding who Jesus is, according to the author. He is the hoped-for Messiah but understood in a very different way from what was usual, not as one who would liberate Israel from its enemies. Rather, he is the Word who was with God from the beginning and who came, in effect, to present God's offer of life. The author has transformed the national hope expressed in the expectation of a Messiah liberator like David and bringing good news for the poor to become something of universal significance. Jesus brings the offer of life in relationship with God. This is the heart of what the author sees as the gospel, which he will bring as a constant theme in many variations in the chapters that follow.

Reflection: What does it mean to be the Messiah, according to the author's portrait of Jesus?

The Old and the New (John 2:1–22)

Listening to John

2:1 On the third day there was a wedding in Cana of Galilee, and Jesus' mother was there. **2** Jesus and his disciples had also been invited to the wedding. **3** And when the wine ran out, Jesus' mother said to him, "They don't have any wine."

4 Jesus said to her, "What's that got to do with us, woman? My hour has not yet come."

5 His mother told the servants, "Do whatever he tells you."

6 Now there were six stone pitchers of water sitting there used for purification by the Jews, each with a capacity of two or three measures (20–30 gallons; 75–110 liters). **7** Jesus told them, "Fill the pitchers with water; fill them right up to the top." **8** Then he told them, "Draw some out and take it to the chief steward."

They did so **9** and when the chief steward tasted the water which had been turned into wine and had no idea where it came from—though the servants who had drawn the water out knew—the chief steward called the bridegroom **10** and said to him, "Everyone serves the best wine first and when people are drunk, that's when they serve the inferior wine, but you have kept the best wine till now."

11 Jesus did this first of his miracles in Cana of Galilee and showed his glory for all to see, and his disciples came to faith in him.

12 After that he went down to Capernaum, he and his mother and his brothers along with his disciples, and stayed there for quite some time. **13** The Passover of the Jews was approaching, and Jesus went off up to Jerusalem. **14** And in the temple he found people selling cattle and sheep and doves and currency-exchange personnel at their tables, **15** and, making a whip from cords, he drove them all out of the temple, both the sheep and cattle, and spilled the money of the currency exchange operators and upended their tables, **16** and said to those selling doves, "Take these things away from here! Don't turn my Father's house into a market!"

¹⁷ His disciples remembered that it stands written, "Zeal for your house will consume me."

¹⁸ So the Jews in response said to him, "What sign can you show us that warrants your doing these things?"

¹⁹ Jesus replied and told them, "Destroy this temple and in three days I will raise it up."

²⁰ So the Jews said, "The rebuild of this temple took forty-six years and you're going to raise it up again in three days?" ²¹ But he was talking about the temple of his body. ²² Accordingly, when he was raised from the dead, his disciples remembered that he had said this and came to believe the Scripture and the statement which Jesus had made.

Thinking About John

What a story! Making wine from water to keep the party going! If we found it anywhere else, we would shake our heads at someone providing such a huge quantity of wine to people already drunk. Outrageous and irresponsible! But the author had come across such a story told about Jesus, which put Jesus up there with the best of gods and heroes who could magically turn water into wine. It was in his collection of miracles, and, for all our disbelief, the author would probably have deemed it would have happened.

At the same time, as we shall see, he was anything but happy with stories like this told to wow people into faith. His strategy was to develop them for symbolic meaning, to shift people's attention to what really mattered. There are many clues that this was his intent. To begin with, the amount of wine is enormous: in total, the six vessels contained something like 120–180 gallons/450–665 liters! They could drown in it. This very big wink surely tells the listeners to look beyond the literal meaning.

There are many other small details which suggest deeper meaning. Even the statement in 2:1 that this happened on the third day after he spoke in 1:51 of his death and exaltation! Listeners might think of his resurrection on the third day, to which the author refers later in the chapter. Similarly, his mother's instruction to the servant that they should do whatever he tells them to do would remind them that they as servants should do whatever Jesus commands them. The comment about not knowing where the wine came from is a favorite of the author's, to allude to where Jesus came from as the Word. The servants in the Jesus community know that all very well, a reality the author hints at by his aside.

Keeping the best wine to last has its meaning in the story, but for listeners it would remind them that there is a sequence in God's gifts and that Jesus is the climax, God's greatest gift, as the author has just reminded them in 1:16–17. Authors played with numbers, so that it is also highly probable that the same point is being made with the indication that there were six pitchers. Seven was the number of completion, perfection. Six falls just short. In Jesus perfection, fulfillment, has come. That is the author's message throughout. Here, there remain six pitchers, but changing the water for purification into wine represents the fulfillment.

Wine and weddings have a long history as powerful symbols. One way of giving expression to hope was to picture it as a great feast, like a wedding feast. Elsewhere we have Jesus' parable of the great feast retold as a great wedding feast (Matt 22:1–14). Such big celebratory meals were rare and something a community would look forward to. A feast lent itself well to being an image of hope and salvation, a symbol of both inclusion and of being adequately fed, good news for the poor.

Wine was also connected to celebration. Mark has Jesus speak of the future when he would drink wine again with his disciples (Mark 14:25). He does that in the context of his last meal where he blessed and broke bread and shared a cup of wine, identifying it with his self-giving in love (Mark 14:22–24). Sensitized to the story's symbolic message, listeners would very likely make a connection between this story and their celebration of Holy Communion. In John 6 the author shows that Holy Communion played a significant part in the author's community.

> Those who eat my flesh and drink my blood have eternal life, and
> I will raise them up on the last day; for my flesh is true food, and
> my blood is true drink. (6:54–55)

Far from making the magic of turning water into wine his focus, the author invites his listeners to celebrate who Jesus is and what he brings: the future celebration of new life and the celebration of that life now.

The exchange between Jesus and his mother seems rather harsh as we read it in English, where he addresses his mother with the word, "Woman." A harsh sense is probably not the intent. We find it used similarly when Jesus addresses his mother while hanging on the cross when he links her with the beloved disciple: "Woman, here is your son" (19:26) and elsewhere in addressing others and clearly not in a negative way (4:21; 20:13, 15). The intent therefore is clearly not to be harsh or rude.

His words "My hour has not yet come" in his exchange with her in our story seems at first unrelated to the context, until we recognize that this serves as another clue that the author is pointing to the deeper meaning that the passage celebrates, namely the celebration of life in the community of the faithful after Jesus' death. Indeed, the author often has Jesus speak of his "hour" when using the ideas associated with the Son of Man title, referring to his death, exaltation, and return to the Father and sending of the Spirit into the community of faith. He has just done so in 1:51.

If the doctored-up story of making wine from water celebrates the new, the contrast between old and new is even stronger in the episode that follows. The former temple is to be replaced by Jesus, himself, as the author's twisting of Jesus' prediction of the temple's destruction indicates. By the author's time, probably in the 90s CE, the temple had lain in ruins for some twenty or so years, having been destroyed by the Romans in 70 CE. Our story refers to the fact that by Jesus' time it had been undergoing a rebuild for forty-six years, initiated by Herod the Great, and resulting in one of the empire's most famous buildings.

Jews needed to come to terms with its absence, and those far from the homeland had needed to do so already for much of the time, few being able to afford to go on pilgrimage to Jerusalem. Even if the temple was gone, the Law remained and provided the way to live in harmony with God. John's creative reworking not only has Jesus now carrying the Law's function as the greater gift to which it pointed forward (1:16–17), but also has Jesus be the new temple. There was precedent for this in Mark, who portrays the resurrected Jesus as the stone upon which the new temple, the community of faith, would be built (Mark 12:10–11).

As is typical in John's Gospel, we have layers of meaning and beneath them older tradition. Mark brings Jesus' action in the temple as a provocative event of his last days. That is most likely when it took place and formed one of the reasons why Jesus was arrested. The allusion to Scripture in John's story still reflects that context: zeal for God's house would indeed consume him, get him into serious trouble, citing Psalm 69:9. It was most likely the context of the saying variously preserved in which Jesus predicted the temple's demise, which according to Mark formed part the charge against him in his Jewish trial (Mark 14:58). Already Mark had expanded the story of

Jesus' action, including having Jesus connect it to the hope for the inclusion of gentiles (Mark 11:15–17).

If we probe behind the accounts we have, it appears that this was act not primarily an attempt at reforming temple procedures, such as moving the necessary provision for purchase of animals for sacrifice and for currency exchange from its huge outer court. (They needed the exchange to enable people to make their contribution in the currency of Tyrian shekels as the temple required.) It appears rather to have been a prophetic act symbolizing the temple's impending destruction, a reading of the fate it would inevitably face but seeing that fate as God's judgment, hence the controversial saying.

It seems therefore very probable that the author has decided to relocate the event away from Jesus' last days and to insert it right here at the beginning. It serves him well for the theme of the new replacing the old. Behind his version may well be older tradition. Mark has Jesus attack the temple leadership for its exploitation of the vulnerable (Mark 12:38–44). John's tradition focuses on the commerce, but suggesting it was out of place rather than corrupt. In common is the action.

Realistically, an undertaking to clear out all the animals would seem improbable, both because the area of the outer court was huge, the size of something like six football fields, and crowded, and because it was carefully watched over by the Roman detachment that was stationed in Jerusalem from Caesarea for the festival. Mark suggests only that Jesus upends the currency exchange tables and the seats of those selling doves and interferes with those carrying things through the temple (Mark 11:15–16). Such a symbolic act, quickly done, after which Jesus could disappear into the crowd, seems the most likely scenario.

For John and his listeners these two episodes speak to their faith as a community celebrating new life and engaged in true worship in the new temple that is Christ and his community.

Reflection: In what ways can this chapter inform our understanding of worship today?

Born from Above (John 2:23—3:36)

Listening to John

2:23 While he was in Jerusalem at the Festival of the Passover, many came to believe in him, seeing the miracles he was performing. **24** Jesus, himself, however, did not believe in them because he knew all people **25** and had no need to have anyone testify about a person, because he, himself, knew what was going on in a person.

3:1 Now there was a person, one of the Pharisees, called Nicodemus, who was a leader of the Jews. **2** He came to him by night and said to him, "Rabbi, we know that you have come as a teacher from God, because no one can do the miracles you do unless God is with him."

3 In reply Jesus said to him, "Truly, truly I tell you, unless someone is born from above, they cannot see the kingdom of God."

4 Nicodemus said to him. "How can a person who is old be born? Surely, they can't enter their mother's womb a second time and be born, can they?"

5 Jesus answered, "Truly, truly, I tell you, unless someone is born by water and the Spirit they cannot enter the kingdom of God. **6** What is born of flesh is flesh, and what is born of the Spirit is spirit. **7** Don't be surprised that I told you, you must be born from above. **8** Wind blows where it wants to and you hear its sound, but you don't know where it has come from nor where it is going. So it is with someone born of the Spirit."

9 Nicodemus in reply said to him, "How can this be?"

10 In response Jesus said to him, "Are you Israel's teacher yet you don't know these things? **11** Truly, truly I tell you, we are talking of what we know and testifying to what we have seen, and you don't accept our testimony. **12** If I've told you earthly things and you don't believe, how will you believe if I tell you heavenly things? **13** And no one has gone up into heaven except the one who came down from heaven, the Son of Man. **14** And as Moses lifted up the snake in the outback, so the Son of Man must be lifted up, **15** so that all who believe in him may have eternal life. [16] For God loved the world so much that he gave up his only Son, so that all who believe in him may not perish but have eternal life. [17] For God did not send his Son into the world to condemn the world, but so that the world might be saved through him. [18] Anyone believing in him is not condemned, but anyone not believing stands condemned because they have not believed in the name of the only Son of God. [19] And this is the judgment, that light has come into the world and people loved darkness rather than light, because their deeds were evil. [20] All who do bad things hate the light and don't come to the light, lest their deeds be exposed. [21] Those who do the truth come to the light in order that their deeds may be shown up, namely as having been done under God."

[22] After this, Jesus and his disciples went into the Judean countryside, and there he spent time with them and was baptizing. [23] John, too, was baptizing in Aenon near Salim, because there was lots of water there, and people came and were being baptized. [24] For John had not yet been put in prison. [25] So a discussion developed between some of John's disciples and a Jew about purification. [26] And they came to John and said to him, "Rabbi, the fellow who was with you on the other side of the Jordan, about him you testified, look, he's performing baptisms, and everyone is going to him."

[27] In response, John said to them, "No one can receive authorization unless it is granted them from heaven. [28] You, yourselves, can confirm that I said I am not the Messiah, but that I have been sent in advance of another. [29] The one with the bride is the bridegroom. The bridegroom's friend is the one standing by and listening and who is filled with joy when he hears the voice of the bridegroom. Accordingly, this is the moment when my joy has been fulfilled. [30] He must become the significant one, and I must become less so."

[31] The one who comes from above is above all. The one from the earth belongs to the earth and speaks of the earth. The one who comes from heaven [32] bears witness to what he has seen and heard, and no one accepts his testimony. [33] But anyone who does accept his testimony sets his seal on the fact God is reliable. [34] For the one whom God sent speaks the words of God, because he doesn't just have the Spirit in a partial way. [35] The Father loves the Son and has put all things into his

hands. ³⁶ Those who believe in the Son have eternal life, but those who fail to trust the Son will not see life, but God's anger rests on them.

Thinking About John

As we move from the two episodes of chapter 2 into chapter 3, we encounter the skills and concerns of the author at their best. I have chosen to attach 2:23–25 closely to what follows in chapter 3 because it clearly belongs there as an introduction. It makes a striking claim. People believed in Jesus, and Jesus didn't believe in them! Why? Because they believed in Jesus on the basis of his miracles, and for the author that fails to grasp who Jesus is. It is not that the author, as a person of his time, doubted miracles. It was rather that he saw an approach to winning followers for Jesus primarily on the basis of his miracles, the wow factor, as an aberration.

In a world where there were competing claims for authority made by teachers and politicians based on alleged miracles, it was inevitable that Jesus was presented by some in the same way. Believe in him! He could do marvels. Emperors engaged in such propaganda, too. It is interesting that the problem appears to have been relatively widespread as the Jesus movement developed. Paul had to confront it in writing to the congregations in Corinth, reminding them so eloquently that love is the mark of the Spirit:

> If I speak in the tongues of mortals and of angels, but do not have love, I am a noisy gong or a clanging cymbal. And if I have prophetic powers, and understand all mysteries and all knowledge, and if I have all faith, so as to remove mountains, but do not have love, I am nothing. (1 Cor 13:1–2)

Similarly, Matthew pictures Jesus predicting how many might call him Lord but completely miss the point:

> Not everyone who says to me, "Lord, Lord," will enter the kingdom of heaven, but only one who does the will of my Father in heaven. On that day many will say to me, "Lord, Lord, did we not prophesy in your name, and cast out demons in your name, and do many deeds of power in your name?" Then I will declare to them, "I never knew you; go away from me, you evildoers." (Matt 5:21–23)

Matthew reinforces the theme in his image of judgment day for sheep and goats (25:31–46). Both groups call the judge "Lord," but the goats are exposed as missing what he was on about. Our author comes back to the theme in John 4:48 where he complains that people want signs and wonders to be able to believe and in 6:14–15 where Jesus absented himself when he realized that people wanted to crown him Messiah based on his miracles. In chapter 7, he has Jesus' brothers suggest he win admirers through his miracles and the author declares them unbelievers (7:5), because they fail to understand Jesus' priorities.

John makes a link between 2:23–25 and the story of Nicodemus by repeating the Greek word we have translated with "person" (*anthropos*): Jesus "had no need to have anyone testify about a *person*, because he, himself, knew what was going on in a *person*. "Now there was a *person*, one of the Pharisees, called Nicodemus" (3:1). As a result, the author has Nicodemus serve as an example of the faith Jesus does not want. Thus, Nicodemus expresses this inadequate faith: "Rabbi, we know that you have come as a teacher from God, because no one can do the miracle you do unless God is with him" (3:2). Jesus challenges Nicodemus to consider true faith, insisting that if he is to see what the kingdom of God is about, he needs a completely new start: he must be born from above!

It is typical of the author to play with double meanings. The affirmation by Nicodemus, "Rabbi, we know that you have come as a teacher from God, because no one can do the miracles you do unless God is with him," is inadequate at one level. It is, however, very adequate at another level if understood in the light of what the author has said about Jesus from the beginning. He is, indeed, the Son sent by the Father, as the author's listeners will well know. This is one of many occasions when they will smile.

The author has already introduced the imagery of being born when he talks about those who received the Word, who gained the right to be called God's children, who were "born not of blood, nor of the will of the flesh, nor of the will of a male, but from God" (1:12–13). It was a way of speaking of a new beginning. Paul, for instance, depicts our coming to faith as an act in which God adopts us as children: "And because you are children, God has sent the Spirit of his Son into our hearts, crying, 'Abba! Father!'" (Gal 4:6); "For you did not receive a spirit of slavery to fall back into fear, but you have received a spirit of adoption. When we cry, 'Abba! Father!'" (Rom 8:15).

At this point, the author is developing a dramatic scene that he will use finally to answer the key question: What then is true faith? The figure, Nicodemus, serves as a caricature of those who fail to find true faith. The author's playfulness is apparent again in Jesus' initial answer where he uses the word *anothen*, which can mean "from above" or "again" (a play on words that possibly only works in Greek, and so, is likely to be part of the author's creativity). The character Nicodemus is depicted, indeed, as particularly dumb and dense. This is a drama and is larger than life. So he has Nicodemus ask stupid questions, like thinking Jesus meant "again" instead of "from above." In an almost cruel caricature, the author holds Nicodemus as Israel's teacher up to ridicule. This is a kind of serious and playful faith entertainment designed to elicit smiles and maybe smirks from listeners and not to be read as history.

The author links "from above," and so by implication its contrast with "from below," to the contrast between flesh and Spirit. Nicodemus' absurd question has him talking of physical birth, but he is also a caricature of a faith that concerns itself with rituals and rites at an earthly level, already symbolized in the six stone jars and not least in the temple. The author portrays Jesus as wanting to engage people in what he sees as reality, which belongs above or, better, belongs to the realm of the Spirit. Life in relationship with God is the theme. One begins, is born into this life, by believing Jesus and, in particular, by accepting the offer of a relationship which he brings on God's behalf.

We meet the author's playfulness also in his use of the word Spirit, which in Greek (and also in Hebrew) can also mean breath or wind. He plays with the idea of wind in 3:8. In other words, the author is promoting faith as a relationship focused not on earthly realities, such as cult and temple, but on God as Spirit.

With all this, Nicodemus is depicted as hopelessly lost. At one level, this is entertainment for John's listeners, who might well have laughed as they pictured the scene, like a stage comedy, but it was also more serious because the author then takes them beyond the scene to bring out the real significance of Jesus as he sees it. From 3:11 onwards we effectively leave the stage play with Nicodemus behind and the author starts having Jesus speak not to Nicodemus alone but to all like him, using "you" in the plural. In effect, we are from this point on hearing the author speak about Jesus.

The contrast in 3:12 between earthly things of which Jesus spoke and heavenly things is best seen not as a contrast between whatever Jesus might have just said about earthly realities and spiritual realities, but between Jesus' earthly ministry and the events surrounding his death and resurrection which he is about to relate. It recalls the contrast in 1:50-51 where Jesus tells Nathanael there is something even more important to be seen.

Here the focus therefore shifts to Jesus' death and his return to God, expressed as exaltation, and ascension. Again, we have a wordplay in the use of the word, translated "lifted up," because it can mean literally being lifted up and also being exalted. The eyes of the world will see Jesus lifted up onto a cross. The eyes of faith will see this as the beginning of his being exalted to return to be with God. In 3:13 we have reference to his going back up, his ascending, and in 3:14 a reference to his being lifted up, exalted.

The lifting up makes eternal life possible. That is repeated in the famous John 3:16. In speaking of God giving or giving up his Son (meaning giving him up to death) the author is portraying his death and exaltation as the basis for making the gift of eternal life available to all. This would tap into the widespread tradition that depicted Jesus' death as like a sacrifice for sins. The author certainly employs that tradition elsewhere, such as when he speaks of Jesus as the good shepherd giving up his life for the sheep.

It should not however be pressed to the point where we have to imagine that the author assumed that before his death Jesus was not able to offer eternal life and that every time he appears to do so it has to be read as promising something people would have to wait for until after his death. That is clearly not the case. He is the Word incarnate, already the source of life and salvation during his ministry. The author has the flexibility to use both ways of expressing this offer of life. It would have helped that indeed for most of his listeners this message of life would have reached them well after Easter as a result of the mission that the Spirit, given by God after Jesus' departure, made possible. Already the author's words in 3:19-21 about life coming into the world indicate how he can hold both ideas together.

The emphasis on love in the famous John 3:16 is repeated in a different way in what follows. God was not wanting to condemn but to save! The author then brings what has by this point become a speech of Jesus or perhaps, better, the author's speech about him and its consequences: believe it and you escape judgment; don't believe it and you will face condemnation. Those are the stark alternatives.

In 3:19-21 the author provides a rationale for the two responses. Good people respond because they are good. Bad people do not, because they are bad. They are not bad as a result of not believing. They are bad to begin with. Some would find comfort in such an explanation. If taken literally, it would seem to assume a closed system. Some people are good, and some people are bad, and that is that. Such a belief system assumes some people are simply to be written off, a terrible contradiction of a gospel of love. In reality, however, the author assumes that bad people (indeed, who does not qualify!) can turn to God for forgiveness. It is, for the author, not a closed system.

We shall find similar explanations later, which declare some people destined to believe and some people destined not to believe, only to find that these statements were never meant to be pressed literally, and John always assumed that people could change their minds. And, by speaking in this way John never assumed that those who refused to believe couldn't help it and should be absolved of any guilt, as though their decision was out of their control.

Following the scene with Nicodemus and the author's extrapolations, we return in 3:22–30 to John the Baptist, where once again the author clearly wants to make sure people put John in his appropriate place. It is uncertain whether the account rests on history when it reports John and Jesus overlapping for a while. The claim that Jesus was baptizing more people than John may well be part of the author's agenda of putting John in his place. The Synoptic Gospels have Jesus begin his ministry only after John was arrested (e.g., Mark 1:14). Unlike John, they do not have Jesus baptizing. The author may be aware of this when in 4:2, somewhat unconvincingly, he inserts a correction to say that it was Jesus' disciples who were baptizing. Probably there was some overlap.

The author, however, has used what was possibly authentic tradition about overlap to reinforce his point about John, when he then has John use the imagery of a wedding night to depict his subordinate role. Jesus is the bridegroom. He is just the best man, expected to announce with acclamation when the marriage had been consummated, such as they apparently did. The author is reinforcing the message he was giving to disciples of John the Baptist of his time: listen to John and join the Jesus movement!

There is no clear end to John the Baptist's statements, so it is possible to read 3:31–36 as also his words. Alternatively, we have another case, as earlier in 3:11, of the author drifting into making his own statements. This is more likely. The contrast returns to above and below, heavenly and earthly, as in the exchange with Nicodemus. Jesus is the one who has come from above. God has given him the Spirit, an allusion to Jesus' baptism, and done so not partially but fully. He has also authorized him, expressed as giving things into his hands. The author then returns to the stark alternatives he earlier outlined between those who believe in Jesus and receive eternal life and those who reject Jesus and face God's anger in judgment.

This closing section acts in some ways as a summary of the author's message. Jesus is clearly God's agent on earth so that a response to him is a response to God. In that sense he is God's envoy, sent by God, and carries the authority attributed to such envoys (who represent the sender) in the ancient world. When the author employs this image of Jesus as being God's envoy, he has him function differently from most envoys, because he comes not to provide information, beside the basic fact that he is truly authorized and sent, but to offer a relationship on God's behalf, an offer of life. This becomes the constant theme in John's Gospel, like the melody repeating itself over and over again in many variations in a symphony.

Reflection: What was the author's concern about miracles?

The Water of Life (John 4:1–54)

Listening to John

4:1 When Jesus learned that the Pharisees had heard that Jesus was gaining and baptizing more disciples than John—**2** though in fact Jesus himself was not baptizing them but rather his disciples—**3** he left Judea and set off again for Galilee.

4 And he had to pass through Samaria. **5** Accordingly, he came to a village in Samaria called Sychar, near the parcel of land which Jacob gave to his son Joseph. **6** And Jacob's well was there. So Jesus, being exhausted from his journey, was sitting there by the well and it was about midday. **7** One of the Samaritan women comes along to draw water and Jesus says to her, "Give me some to drink!"

8 For the disciples had gone off into the village to buy food. **9** The Samaritan woman says to him, "How come you, a Jew, are asking me, a Samaritan woman, for a drink?" For Jews don't share vessels with them.

10 In reply Jesus told her, "If you knew the gift of God and who it is who's asking you to give him a drink, you would have asked him, and he would have given you living water."

11 She said to him, "Sir, you don't have anything to draw water with, and the well is deep. Where are you going to get living water? **12** You don't think you're greater than our father, Jacob, do you, who gave us the well from which he himself drank and his sons and offspring?"

13 In response Jesus told her, "Everyone drinking from this water will get thirsty again. **14** But whoever drinks of the water that I supply them will never be thirsty ever again, but the water that I supply will become in them a spring of water bubbling up for eternal life."

15 The woman said to him, "Sir, give me this water, so I won't be thirsty and won't need to come here to draw water."

16 He said to her, "Go and call your husband and come back here."

17 In response the women told him, "I haven't got a husband."

Jesus said to her, "Well spoken, 'I haven't got a husband', [18] because you've had five husbands, and now the one you have isn't your husband. You've told the truth."

[19] The woman then said to him. "Sir, I see you're a prophet. [20] Our fathers worshipped on this mountain, but you say that Jerusalem is the place where one should worship."

[21] Jesus said to her, "Believe me, woman, the hour is coming when you will worship the Father neither on this mountain nor in Jerusalem. [22] You worship what you do not know; we worship what we know, because salvation comes from the Jews. [23] But the hour is coming and is already here when true worshippers will worship the Father in spirit and in truth. For the Father is looking for people like that to worship him. [24] God is spirit and those worshipping him need to do so in spirit and in truth."

[25] The woman said to him, "I know the Messiah, called the Christ, is coming. When he comes, he will teach us everything."

[26] Jesus told her, "I'm that one, talking to you."

[27] And at this point his disciples returned and were surprised that he was talking to a woman. However, none of them said, "What do you want with her or why are you talking with her?"

[28] The woman left behind her pitcher and went off into the village and told people, [29] "Come and see this person who told me all I have ever done. Could he be the Messiah?" [30] They came out from the village and approached him.

[31] In the meantime his disciples were questioning him, telling him, "Rabbi, eat something!"

[32] But he told them, "I have food to eat which you don't know about."

[33] The disciples were saying to each other, "No one brought him anything to eat, did they?"

[34] Jesus said to them, "My food is to do the will of the one who sent me and to finish his work. [35] Don't you say, in four months there'll be a harvest. Look, I tell you, lift up your eyes and see the fields; they're white already, ripe for harvesting. [36] The one who reaps is getting his pay and is gathering fruit for eternal life, so that both the sower and the harvester can be glad. [37] In this the saying proves itself true: 'One sows,

and another reaps.' ³⁸ I sent you to reap what you had not toiled to sow. Others did the sowing and you have entered into their toil."

³⁹ Many Samaritans from that village came to believe in him because of the woman's testimony, that he had told her all that she ever did. ⁴⁰ As the Samaritans approached him, they were asking him to stay around with them; and he did stay for two days. ⁴¹ Many more came to faith in him because of his message, ⁴² and were saying to the woman, we believe now not just because of your report, but because we have heard him for ourselves and know that he is truly the savior of the world.

⁴³ After two days he left there for Galilee. ⁴⁴ For Jesus, himself, testified that a prophet gets no respect in his home territory. ⁴⁵ When therefore he came to Galilee, the Galileans welcomed him, having seen everything that he had done in Jerusalem at the festival, for they had been to the festival.

⁴⁶ He arrived again in Cana of Galilee, where he had changed water into wine. And there was a certain royal official, whose son in Capernaum was sick. ⁴⁷ When he heard that Jesus had come there from Judea to Galilee, he went to him and asked him to come down and heal his son, because he was on the point of dying. ⁴⁸ Jesus accordingly said to him, "Unless you lot see signs and wonders you won't believe!"

⁴⁹ The royal official said to him, "Sir, come on down before my child dies!"

⁵⁰ Jesus said to him, "Go, your son is alive."

And the man believed the word that Jesus spoke to him and went off. ⁵¹ While he was already on his way down, his slaves met him and said, "Your son's alive."

⁵² So he found out from them at what time he started to get better. They told him, "Yesterday at one o'clock the fever left him." ⁵³ The father accordingly knew that this was precisely the time when Jesus told him, "Your son is alive," and he came to faith along with his whole household.

⁵⁴ Jesus performed this second miracle having returned from Judea to Galilee.

Thinking About John

The chapter has a rather awkward start. It again depicts Jesus as outdoing John, part of the author's agenda, but then corrects the statement by saying that it was only his disciples who baptized. The chapter then takes off with its dramatic scene of Jesus and the Samaritan woman. It is a seriously playful celebration of the author's central message, expressed here by portraying Jesus as the one who offers the gift of the water of life.

Behind the author's dramatic scene is very probably a kernel of memory that has Jesus doing something which we know was rather typical of his actions. He crossed a boundary not normally crossed, namely as a Jew being willing to drink water taken from a Samaritan's pitcher of water. Such a pitcher might be suspected to be ritually unclean and so should be avoided. More than that, he was talking with a woman out in public and, perhaps as the following dialogue indicates, also a woman with a bad reputation. Respectable men don't chat with women in a public place like that, according to best practice of the day, let alone one who has a reputation.

The fact that it happens at a well may be part of the original story or may be more playfulness. For meetings between men and women at wells were famous for leading to marriages, such as those of Isaac and Rebekah and Moses and Zipporah. This, however, is no romance. It is drama inviting audience involvement. The audience is meant to laugh or at least smile when the woman completely misses the point of Jesus' offer of living water, thinking he meant real water which would relieve her of her daily trip to the well. Laugh!

Typical of the author's employment of double meaning, living water can mean fresh or flowing rather than still water, but Jesus means something quite different. The next laugh or smile comes when she says, "You don't think you're greater than our father, Jacob, do you?" Of course he is! Laugh again!

The shift in 4:16 to the subject of the woman's husbands may at one level be filling out the picture of the woman as likely in those times to have had a bad reputation, but the author may be using it symbolically to depict what many Jews saw as Samaritans' flirtation with idolatry, a sin often depicted in marital terms as adultery. The tradition and probably the author's Jewish prejudices are reflected in the claim that the line of salvation comes through the Jews, not the Samaritans. The author has Jesus, however, do what in a sense he had done in chapter 2 with the stone jars and the temple, namely make the claim that from now on true worship would not be tied to places and temples but would be spiritual.

We are in for our next laugh or smile when the woman ponders, could this be the Messiah? He's just told her that he is! What was she thinking! Even more, then she declares why: because he told her all that she ever did! Laugh again! Some will have been sure to connect that to her having had five husbands, the only thing Jesus told her about herself. Her stumbling figure crosses the stage before us and eventually models true discipleship: for she goes and tells others to come.

The author slips in the disciples' return and their surprise that he is there talking to a woman, perhaps an echo of an original event. Jesus crosses the barriers of prejudice over gender and over culture. Amid the author's celebration of Jesus as giver of the water of life we must not forget this broader commitment to affirming difference.

The author is at play again in having the disciples and Jesus pass like ships in the night. They are talking about real food. He is talking about food metaphorically. Typically, the author slides into having Jesus talk about later times, reflecting very probably on the success of the later mission to Samaritans, the harvest.

The author then takes us to the Samaritan villagers. Was it a put down that they told the woman they believed because they had heard for themselves and not because of her report? Perhaps not. Certainly, their acclamation that Jesus is the savior of the world highlights that the gospel is to reach out to all. Ultimately it was the woman who made it possible.

That acclamation may also function as a transitional thought to the next short episode. We know the story as the healing of the gentile centurion's slave in Capernaum, preserved in Matthew and Luke and linked to the promise of inclusion of gentiles (Matt 8:5–13; Luke 7:1–10). Our author calls him a royal official, which would mean he was associated with the court of Herod Antipas, but does not draw attention to the likelihood that he was gentile. Does he assume his hearers would understand it this way?

The author is using a form of the story that has been told in a way to emphasize the miraculous: healed at exactly the time Jesus spoke! Wow! Many of the author's miracle stories show signs of having had their impact ramped up for effect. Having the healing occur not in Capernaum where the child was but from further away in Cana also enhances the effect. The fact that the author talks of a son whereas the parallel story speaks of a slave may seem a major difference, until we recognize that the word used for a child could also mean slave, so this probably explains the difference.

The author's distinctive contribution does not question the miraculous—he was a man of his time—but does restate his concern about such faith when he has Jesus almost rebuke the man by saying, "Unless you lot see signs and wonders you won't believe!" The "you" in this statement is not singular but plural, hence my translation, "you lot." The rebuke is clearly intended for a wider audience, including all listening to John's Gospel. John knows that people believed in Jesus because of such miracles. His sources said so. But he was also keen to point out that this can easily lead to people missing the point of Jesus' mission, which was to offer a relationship with God in which they would find true life, expressed in this chapter as the water of life. It was not to wow people with wonders.

This is the first in a series of instances where the author uses images drawn from key aspects of human experience that have universal appeal. Here, what lies behind the image of water is the notion of thirst. The author is presenting Jesus—or, better, God through Jesus—as able to quench the deep inner thirst that is a universal need. His next instance in the series is the image of bread in John 6 and is used to address deep hunger that can be satisfied through a relationship with God as Jesus presents God. There follow images of light and life, again, universal images reflecting human need, and portraying God as able to meet these deep human needs.

Unlike with the images of bread, light, and life, the author does not have Jesus declare "I am the living water," as he does in having Jesus declare he is the bread, light, life. Instead, he portrays Jesus offering it. In all instances the author is not saying that Jesus is in himself bread, light, and life, as if he is these things independent of God. Rather, he is these things because and only because ultimately it is *God* who meets these deep existential needs.

Reflection: Jesus crosses more than one boundary. Which boundaries? And where do you see them today?

2

Claims Contested

Resurrection Now (John 5:1–47)

Listening to John

5:1 After this there was a festival of the Jews and Jesus went up to Jerusalem. **2** In Jerusalem there is a pool near the sheepgate, called Bethzatha in Hebrew, and it has five colonnades. **3** Lying among these was a crowd of people who were sick or blind or lame or paralyzed. **5** And a certain fellow had been there beset with his illness for thirty-eight years. **6** Jesus saw him lying there and knew that he had been there already for a long time and said to him, "Do you want to be made well?"

7 The ill man answered, "Sir I don't have anyone to put me into the pool when its waters stir. When I approach, someone else gets there ahead of me."

8 Jesus said to him, "Get up, pick up your mat and walk!" **9** And immediately the man became well and picked up his mat and began to walk.

Now that day was a Sabbath. **10** So Jews began to say to the man who had been healed, "It's the Sabbath, so you're not allowed to be carrying your mat."

11 He replied, "The man who made me well, he told me. 'Take up your mat and walk.'"

12 They asked him, "Who was this fellow who told you, 'Take it up and walk'?"

¹³ The man who had been healed did not know who it was, because Jesus had disappeared into the crowd that was there.

¹⁴ Then later, Jesus found him in the temple and told him, "Look, you've got better, so no more sinning, so you don't end up with something worse happening to you!" ¹⁵ The man went off and told the Jews that it was Jesus who had made him better. ¹⁶ Because of this the Jews started hounding Jesus for doing such things on the Sabbath.

¹⁷ In response Jesus told them, "My Father has kept on working right up to now, and I'm working, too."

¹⁸ Because of this the Jews went after him wanting all the more to kill him, not only because he broke the Sabbath, but also because he was talking about God as his own father, making himself equal to God.

¹⁹ So, to counter this, Jesus said, "Truly, truly, I tell you, the Son can do nothing except what he sees his Father doing. What he does, that's similarly what the Son also does. ²⁰ For the Father loves the Son and shows him everything he is doing, and greater deeds than these will he show him, so you'll be amazed. ²¹ As the Father raises the dead and brings them to life, so likewise the Son, too, will restore back to life anyone he wants to. ²² For the Father does not judge anyone, but has delegated judging to the Son, ²³ so that all may honor the Son as they honor the Father. Whoever does not honor the Son, does not honor the Father who sent him.

²⁴ Truly, truly, I tell you, anyone hearing my message and believing in the one who sent me has eternal life and won't face condemnation but has passed from death to life. ²⁵ Truly, truly I tell you, the hour is coming and is now here when the dead will hear the voice of the Son of God and those hearing will come back to life. ²⁶ As the Father has life in himself, so also he has granted the Son to have life in himself ²⁷ and has authorized him to conduct judgment because he is the Son of Man. ²⁸ Don't be surprised at this, because the hour is coming when all in the tombs will hear his voice, ²⁹ and those who have done good will come out for resurrection to life, and those who have done evil will face resurrection to be damned.

³⁰ I can't do anything of my own accord. As I hear I judge and my judgment is just, because I am not pursuing my own interests, but the interests of the one who sent me. ³¹ If I were to testify on my own behalf, my testimony would not be reliable. ³² There is another person

who testifies on my behalf, and I know that the testimony he provides on my behalf is reliable. ³³ You sent after John, and he has borne reliable testimony. ³⁴ I don't in fact need testimony from people but I'm telling you these things so that you may be saved. ³⁵ He was a torch burning bright, and you were happy to enjoy his light for a while. ³⁶ I also have testimony weightier than John's, namely the evidence of the deeds that the Father has authorized me to perform. The deeds themselves provide evidence about me, namely that the Father sent me.

³⁷ And the one who sent me, the Father, he has borne testimony on my behalf, but you have never heard his voice nor seen his form. ³⁸ And you don't have his word abiding in you, because you don't believe in the one whom he sent. ³⁹ You search the Scriptures thinking that you will find life in them, but they in fact are testifying about me, ⁴⁰ and you aren't prepared to come to me in order to find life.

⁴¹ I'm not into winning accolades from people, ⁴² but I know what you are like, namely that you don't have the love of God in you. ⁴³ I came in my Father's name, and you don't accept me. If someone else comes in their own name, you will accept them. ⁴⁴ How can you believe, when you're looking to receive accolades from others and aren't looking to receive affirmation from the one and only God? ⁴⁵ Don't imagine I'll be the one accusing you before the Father. It's Moses, the one you set your hope on, who will accuse you. ⁴⁶ Because if you had believed Moses, you would have believed me, because he wrote about me. ⁴⁷ If you won't believe what he wrote, how are you going to believe the message I bring?"

Thinking About John

This next chapter begins with a healing by a pool. At a very early stage someone added in 5:4 an explanation about the pool. It had healing qualities when the waters in it stirred but only enough for the first person in to be healed. The oldest manuscripts did not have this explanation, so we move directly from verse 3 to verse 5. The focus of the story is, in any case, not who got healed in the pool but how a man, presumed lame, finally came to be healed by Jesus.

Jesus heals the man simply by telling him to get up and walk. It is similar to the story in Mark about the paralyzed man let down through the roof (Mark 2:1-12). There, Jesus tells him his sins are forgiven and when criticized, answers: What was easier, to tell him his sins were forgiven or to tell him to a get up, pick up his mat and walk, as here? The similarity extends also to the fact that here in John 5 Jesus assumes the man's plight was because of sins and so tells him not to sin anymore or else he'll find himself in even greater trouble. Was the author in some way rewriting Mark's story or just having Jesus make similar responses?

It was typical of ancient world pathology to attribute what was probably some form of paralysis to sin. It belonged to their worldview. In John 9, which also has a healing, we find Jesus not attributing the man's blindness to sin. We today have benefitted from generations of medical research which helps us to understand that illness and paralysis can have a variety of causes and we rightly do not attribute such ills to a person's sinfulness.

Guilt may sometimes affect health and wellbeing, but the causes are much more likely to lie elsewhere. Sometimes people facing illness or disability can blame themselves or at least embrace the notion that they somehow deserve it. In some instances, they may, but in most instances, part of the healing will be to help people free themselves from putting themselves down and blaming themselves where that itself is not only unwarranted but destructive.

The story becomes a platform for what follows, indeed for the first of many long speeches that the author has Jesus give about himself. The transition from the story to the controversy that generates the speech is the author's note that this healing happened on the Sabbath. The complaint is against what the religious critics see as a breach of Sabbath law by the man when he starts walking along carrying his mat.

The exchange with the critics is similar to what we find in John 9, when the man healed of his blindness on the Sabbath lost sight of where Jesus was. What emerges is that the critics not only condemn the man; they also condemn Jesus for what he did on the Sabbath, recalling other stories which we find in Mark, for instance, of Jesus being criticized for healing on the Sabbath (Mark 3:1-6).

The author has Jesus respond in a way that may reflect awareness of debates in rabbinic circles about work on the Sabbath, especially whether God could be considered to work on the Sabbath. Jesus' response is simple: God works on the sabbath and so do I! That then raises what will have become major issues of dispute between Jews who joined the Jesus movement and those who did not, namely the special status being claimed for Jesus.

Were they being blasphemous, because it often sounded like they were saying Jesus was a second God or God's equal, as here? The choice of the author and his communities to use the image of God's Wisdom/Word to speak about Jesus would have inevitably raised such concerns. The Gospel begins, after all, by declaring that the Word *was* God, while on either side of that statement saying that he was *with* God, a seeming contradiction, which clearly implied that the statement that the Word was God needed some careful unpacking.

Mostly, the author speaks of Jesus as God's Son, much as sometimes Jewish writers had spoken of Wisdom as God's daughter or even as God's companion. We can see in this passage how the author wards off accusations of blasphemy. The choice to identify Jesus with God's Wisdom/Word and speak of him in familial terms as God's Son needed defending. The beginning of this defense was to have the Son deny that he was in any way independent of God. He uses the pattern of sons following their fathers' professions to have Jesus speak of being subordinate and of doing what he had been told to do, namely the things his Father did (5:19).

As in the climax to chapter 1 and also in the exchange with Nicodemus in chapter 3, he has Jesus not only defend his action in the present as commissioned and authorized by God, but also point to greater deeds to come (5:20), in particular, the exercise of judgment. Not surprisingly he speaks of himself in this context as the Son of Man, the figure traditionally expected to be God's agent of judgment.

The author has Jesus juxtapose the present and the future when having Jesus speak of exercising judgment on God's behalf. Traditional future expectation was there would be a resurrection of the dead, the good and the bad, and that the latter would face condemnation and the former rise to eternal life. The author clearly still assumes that future expectation and will later have Jesus speak of it as "the last day" (6:39–40). He does something else, however, which shifts the focus to the present: he has Jesus declare that in effect those who come to receive eternal life from God, through Jesus, have in a sense *already* been resurrected from death to life (5:24). In effect, then, people are facing judgment in the way they respond to Jesus in the present, faith meaning acquittal and disbelief meaning condemnation.

The effect of shifting the main focus to the encounter with Jesus is to make the central focus of hope not a future event but the personal encounter with Jesus. Ultimately what this is really doing is that it puts *God* at the center. The issue is: we have an invitation to life now from God and can choose to accept it or reject it. This is the golden thread running through John's Gospel.

From midway through the chapter the author shifts the focus back to arguments about the legitimacy of the claims he is having Jesus make about himself. This brings us back to John the Baptist, whose role the author has reconfigured to be primarily one of pointing to Jesus (5:32–35). John was indeed a light, as he states here, but never to be seen as competing with Jesus as light.

The next arguments appeal to the evidence of Jesus' deeds (5:36). That evidence is, the author has Jesus assert, even more weighty because it shows him doing God's work, assumed here to be bringing healing and hope. It also puts John the Baptist in his place, as *a* witness, but not as *the* witness. The author also has Jesus appeal to Scripture on the basis of the claim that they legitimize him (5:39). These claims come alongside attacks on the critics, such as that they fail to hear or see who God is and have always done so and that they fail to understand Scripture correctly, thinking that it itself is the source of life.

The allegations include that the critics are bent on winning approval and glory for themselves, instead of resting on God's affirmation and acceptance, and the author has Jesus confront them with the claim that the very Moses whom they intend to honor will be the one to condemn them before God.

The author's composition of this speech as a defense of what he and his community affirm about Jesus will doubtless reflect tensions and conflicts between John's community and other Jewish groups, whether ongoing or in the past. It affirms and it attacks, perhaps in ways that are in danger of generalizing and generating prejudice and anti-Semitism when extracted from the original context of what will have been *inner*-Jewish conflict. It is easier to identify with the positive statements than with the allegations, and even then, we need to see that the claims being made are one model among others for explaining that in Jesus, as the tradition presents him, we are called to a life of faith in relationship with God.

Reflection: How does the author deal with future expectation of resurrection judgment in relating it to the present?

The Bread of Life (John 6:1–71)

Listening to John

6:1 After this Jesus crossed over to the other side of the Sea of Galilee, Lake Tiberias. **2** And a large crowd was following him because they had seen the miraculous healings he had performed for the sick. **3** Jesus went up the hill and was sitting down there with his disciples. **4** It was not long before the Jewish Festival of Passover.

5 Looking up and seeing the large crowd approaching him, Jesus said to Philip, "Where can we buy some bread for them to eat?" **6** He said this to test him for he knew what he was going to do.

7 Philip responded that two hundred denarii wouldn't even be enough for them for everyone to get just a little bit. **8** One of his disciples, Andrew, Simon Peter's brother, then told him, **9** "There's a boy here who's got five barley loaves of bread and two fish, but what's that for such a crowd?"

10 Then Jesus said, "Get people to sit down."

Now there was a lot of green grass in that place. So the men sat down, roughly five thousand in number. **11** Jesus took the loaves and, having given thanks, distributed them to those who were sitting down and did likewise with the fish, as much as they wanted. **12** When they'd had enough, he told his disciples to collect what was left over, so that it wouldn't be lost. **13** They gathered it up and filled twelve baskets from bits of the five barley loaves, which were left over after people had eaten.

14 When people saw the miracle he had performed, they started saying, "This truly is the prophet expected to come into the world." **15** So Jesus, sensing that they were on the brink of coming and grabbing him to make him king, went off up the hill to be all on his own.

16 When evening came, his disciples went down to the lake **17** and, getting into a boat, set off for the other side of the lake to Capernaum. And it was already dark, and Jesus hadn't come to them. **18** And the lake was choppy because there was a strong wind blowing. **19** When they had gone something like twenty-five to thirty stadia [three or four miles; five to seven kilometers], they saw Jesus walking on the lake and coming near the boat, and they were scared. [20] He told them, "It's me. Don't be scared!" [21] They wanted to take him on board, and immediately the boat reached the shore where they were heading.

[22] The next day the crowd that had been located on the other side saw that there'd been just the one boat there, and that Jesus hadn't embarked with his disciples, but the disciples had left on their own. [23] Then some other boats from Tiberias came near to the place where they had eaten when the Lord had given thanks. [24] So when the crowd saw that neither Jesus nor his disciples were any longer there, they got into the boats and set off for Capernaum, looking for Jesus. [25] Finding him over the other side, they said, "Rabbi, how did you get here?"

[26] In response Jesus told them, "Truly, truly, I tell you, you're looking for me not because you saw the miracles [as signs], but because you ate of the loaves and had enough to eat. [27] Put your effort not into getting food that perishes, but food that lasts for eternal life, which the Son of Man will give you. For God the Father has set his seal on him."

[28] They said to him, "What should we do to put our effort into what God wants?"

[29] In reply Jesus said to them, "This is what God wants: that you believe in the one whom he sent."

[30] So they said to him, "What sign then will you do that we can see and so believe in you? What can you do? [31] Our fathers ate manna in the outback, as it is written, 'he gave them food from heaven to eat.'"

[32] Jesus therefore said to them, "Truly, truly I tell you, it was not Moses who gave you bread from heaven but my Father who gives you true bread from heaven. [33] For the bread of God is the one who has come down from heaven and gives life to the world."

[34] So they said to him, "Sir, give us this bread always!"

[35] He said to them, "I am the bread of life. Whoever comes to me will never hunger and whoever believes in me will never thirst. [36] But I'm telling you, you have seen me, and you don't believe. All the Father gives me will come to me [37] and anyone coming to me I certainly won't send them away. [38] For I have come down from heaven not to do my own will, but the will of him who sent me. [39] This is the will of the one who sent me, that of all that he has given me I'll not lose any but will raise them up on the last day. [40] For this is the will of my Father, that

all who see the Son and believe in him may have eternal life, and I will raise them up on the last day."

⁴¹ So the Jews began to complain about him, that he said, "I am the bread come down from heaven," ⁴² and were saying, "Surely this is Jesus, Joseph's son, whose father and mother we know? How can he say, 'I have come down from heaven'?"

⁴³ In response Jesus said, "Don't be complaining among yourselves. ⁴⁴ No one can come to me unless the Father who sent me draws them, and I will raise them up on the last day. ⁴⁵ It is written in the prophets that they shall 'all be taught by God.' Everyone who listens to and learns from the Father comes to me. ⁴⁶ Not that anyone has seen the Father except the one who is from the Father. He has seen the Father. ⁴⁷ Truly, truly, I tell you, anyone who believes has eternal life. ⁴⁸ I am the bread of life. ⁴⁹ Your fathers ate manna in the outback and died. ⁵⁰ This is the bread come down from heaven, so that anyone who eats it will not die. ⁵¹ I am the living bread come down from heaven. If anyone eats of this bread they will live forever. And the bread that I shall give for the life of the world is my flesh."

⁵² The Jews argued among themselves, saying, "How can he give us his flesh to eat?"

⁵³ Jesus said, "Truly, truly, I tell you, unless you eat the flesh of the Son of Man and drink his blood, you have no life in you. ⁵⁴ The one who feeds on my flesh and drinks my blood has eternal life. ⁵⁵ For my flesh is true nourishment, and my blood is true drink. ⁵⁶ The one feeding on my flesh and drinking my blood abides in me and I in them. ⁵⁷ As the living Father sent me, so I live because of the Father, and the one who feeds on me, that one will live because of me. ⁵⁸ This is the bread come down from heaven, not like the way the fathers ate and died. The one who feeds on this bread will live forever."

⁵⁹ He said this while teaching in the Capernaum synagogue. ⁶⁰ Many, accordingly, of his disciples, when they heard this, said, "This claim is hard to take. Who can accept it?"

⁶¹ When Jesus sensed in himself that his disciples were complaining about it, he said to them, "Are you offended by this? ⁶² What if you were to see the Son of Man going back up to where he was before? ⁶³ The spirit is what gives life, the flesh is worth nothing. The words I have spoken to you are spirit and life. ⁶⁴ But there are some

of you not believing. For Jesus knew already from the start that some would not believe in him and who was going to betray him. ⁶⁵ And he was saying, "This is why I told you that no one can come to me except it be granted them by my Father."

⁶⁶ From that point many of his disciples left off from following him and were no longer travelling around with him. ⁶⁷ So Jesus said to the twelve, "You don't want to leave me, too, do you?"

⁶⁸ Simon Peter replied, "Lord, whom should we turn to? You have the words of eternal life. ⁶⁹ And we have come to believe and know that you are the holy one of God."

⁷⁰ Jesus responded: "Did I not choose you twelve? But one of you is a devil."

⁷¹ He was speaking about Judas, son of Simon Iscariot. For he was the one who was going to betray him.

Thinking About John

This is a very long chapter and typical of the author's style. Unlike the other Gospels, which mainly bring relatively short episodes or collections of episodes and sayings, our author starts with material similar to theirs and then develops dialogues and speeches based on it in which Jesus speaks in the language and concepts of the faith of the author's own day. In this way he both connects with the tradition and produces often wonderful images with universal appeal. The fact that Mark had already used the feeding of the five thousand and the four thousand as an image for the good news going to both Jews and gentiles will have encouraged the author of the Fourth Gospel to expand that imagery much further.

We have already noted the image of the water of life. Here he highlights Jesus as the bread of life, just as in chapter 9, starting with the healing of the blind man, he highlights Jesus as the light and in chapter 11, based on the raising of Lazarus, he highlights Jesus as the resurrection and the life.

Here in chapter 6, the starting point is the feeding of the five thousand, a story also found in the other Gospels, and, as in Mark (followed by Matthew and Luke), connected closely to the episode about Jesus walking on the lake. Over the years scholars have pondered whether John drew on Mark or knew an earlier tradition. Most, these days, favor the former explanation. If he is drawing on Mark, he does so very differently from Matthew and Luke, who sometimes follow Mark word for word or with minimal correction or expansion. Our author does his own creative thing.

We mustn't think of him as an author in our terms, as though one day he decided to write a gospel from scratch, as it were. He will have been an active member of a community of faith and will doubtless have told and retold his stories about Jesus many times. When he came to write them down in the form of a gospel, it is also highly likely that over the years he supplemented and developed his text. There are signs of his having done so, more obviously in the final chapters, but many have seen indications of a developing composition here in John 6, especially when the theme of bread is shaped in 6:51–58 by language that probably reflects his community's practice of Holy Communion.

We begin with his starting point: the feeding of the five thousand. It is very similar to Mark's account, even in such details as mentioning two hundred denarii (a denarius was typically a day's wage), though here as not even enough, and twelve baskets of leftovers, already highly symbolic of Israel's twelve tribes. Differences include the naming of the disciples in the conversation, Philip and Andrew, and the addition that Jesus knew all along what he intended to do. John thereby emphasizes that Jesus is in control and knows what he is going to do. The reference to the boy (also a word for servant) and his having barley loaves is also an addition and likely to be a deliberate echo of the story of Elisha's miraculous feeding of a hundred men with barley loaves and his conversation with his servant boy (2 Kgs 4:42–44).

The major addition is in 6:14–15, where the author returns to his concern about miracle-based faith. He had mentioned that the crowd was following Jesus because of the miracles in 6:2. It is just as in 2:23–25, where Jesus does not believe in those who believe in him because of his miracles and in 3:1–3 has Nicodemus illustrate such faith. The encounter with the royal official has Jesus also declare his frustration about people wanting signs and wonders (4:48). Here in 6:14–15 the author has Jesus go for his life from that kind of adulation. That kind of wow-based faith fails to get the message about Jesus' significance.

The author, however, spells out that message and what true faith means only after he tells the story of Jesus' walking on the lake. This story had been told to highlight its miraculous character, as with many of the miracle traditions John used. Not only does Jesus walk on the lake, as in the versions found in Mark and Matthew (Mark 6:45–52; Matt 14:22–33); this version has vamped up the miracles so that the boat suddenly reaches dry land. Wow! As with the story of the feeding, so here, the author brings a corrective to the "wow" faith, when he has Jesus declare, "You're looking for me not because you saw the miracles [as signs], but because you ate of the loaves and got enough to eat" (6:26). That sounds like the opposite: they should have followed because of the miracles, but there is a subtlety here that is not so easily reproduced in English. For the word *semeion* can mean "miracle, sign," as in signs and wonders, but can also mean "sign" in the sense of embodying or pointing to deeper meaning. That is what the author will have Jesus go on to show.

While the author is clearly concerned about miracle-based faith, this does not mean he would not have believed that the miracles took place. His was a world where people were fond of telling such stories of heroes and gods doing magical things. There was a marketplace for claims and counter claims about whom one should follow, based on their miraculous achievements. The author wants none of that kind of propaganda use of miracles. He wants people to go beyond that to see what they represent and symbolize, while still not doubting they took place.

We also need to respect that the author is unlikely to have grappled with the questions that might arise in our minds about such stories. Having the ability to multiply food, why didn't Jesus embark on a mission to feed the hundreds of thousands of people who would have been poor and hungry in his world? The question, put like this, is unfair. This was a one-off event, a story meant to appeal to people to believe in Jesus. It belongs to the discourse of adoration and should not therefore be pressed for its implications in real life. It is also not seen as an ability to be passed on to his disciples let alone the church—much as we would desperately welcome it.

The same might be said of walking on water. What a skill we would like to have in contexts of sea rescue. But that misses the point of such stories. Both the feeding miracle and the walking on water miracle are stories, also richly recalling stories of Israel's past, such as Elisha's feeding or, more significantly, the feeding of Israel by manna in the outback, an image that the author will develop in his dialogue section. The sea miracle would also recall the exodus and the parting of the sea. The author, however, does not want us to stop there. Faith has a much more significant focus.

The dialogue with the crowd, like the dialogue with Nicodemus and the woman at the well, has a touch of serious humor. They want a sign, but as John's hearers well know, Jesus has already given one, namely the feeding of the five thousand! Well may they laugh. Like Moses in the outback, Jesus gave people bread, and here they are asking if he could please give them a sign. He's already given the sign for all to see.

The author then puts the focus squarely on the significance he wants his listeners to recognize in the miracle. It is the sign that Jesus, himself, is the bread come down from heaven, offering life. His comments are not anti-Moses, but they do put Moses in a subordinate position and make very clear: Moses, including the Law of Moses, is not the source of life. Jesus is. As he put it in the previous chapter, the Scriptures, including the Mosaic Law, point forward to Jesus (5:39).

In the declaration, "I am the bread of life. Whoever comes to me will never hunger and whoever believes in me will never thirst" (6:35), the author has Jesus sum up the message thus far and also recalls the image of the water of life celebrated in the encounter with the Samaritan woman in John 4. When the author has them declare, "Give us this bread always!," they are being like the Samaritan woman who thought Jesus was still talking about literal water. They are still thinking literally about bread. Smile again!

As the dialogue continues, the author turns the focus to the problem of rejection, namely those who reject this claim of Jesus and so reject the claim of the author and his communities (6:36–45). If, as is likely, many of them were Jews or converts to Judaism, then having their message be rejected by fellow Jews would have been painful. It would also have been a problem for gentiles who had come to believe that they were now at one with the faith of Israel. Such rejection had the potential to call their faith into question: Have we got it wrong?

This section of the dialogue deals with it by having Jesus claim that God determined who would accept and who would reject him. For some that would be a comfort. They'll not be rejected or disowned. They belong, chosen by God. They could know themselves as being among those destined to accept and be accepted and could see the others as destined not to accept and be accepted. It was all "meant to be," all determined by God. Taken literally, this is a highly problematic claim that at worst writes some people off and, worse, has God write them off. Like much religious language, however, it should not be pressed beyond the way it functions here. If we do press it to its logical conclusion, then those rejecting are predestined to do so and should bear no blame for doing so, but that is far from the author's assumption. Such explanations of who is "in" and who is not, functioned not just to reassure but also to persuade. Perhaps hearing it, they may turn and believe! Coming to terms with rejection is one of the author's concerns to which he regularly returns, next time in John 8.

The author then in 6:41 portrays the Jews as complaining, perhaps intentionally alluding to the way Israel complained in the outback. They inappropriately challenge Jesus' claim to be the bread come down from heaven. After all, they knew his mum and dad. Jesus' response is to repeat the claim about those whom God chooses to respond and those whom he does not. God draws some. Some listen and learn from God. Some don't.

He then has Jesus reaffirm that he is truly the one come down from heaven who can give life. At this point, halfway through 6:51, the author has Jesus start to use different language, perhaps reflecting material with which the author at some stage supplemented his version of Jesus' long speech. Thus far he has had Jesus describe himself as the bread of life and imply that to believe in him is to receive that life. Now he has Jesus put it in terms of his giving his life, a reference to his death.

This introduces a section that therefore frames the message a little differently. You get this life by eating Jesus' flesh and drinking his blood, a rather shocking metaphor. It provokes more complaints from the Jews, not surprisingly. For the author's hearers, however, it was one that made sense because they would hear it as a reference to their celebration of Holy Communion. Body and blood is expressed as flesh and blood but means the same.

It is also interesting that, with the focus shifted to depicting the time after Jesus' death, the author has Jesus speak of himself as the Son of Man again. He regularly has Jesus speak of himself as Son of Man when referring to the events set off by his death, exaltation, glorification, and ascension back to be with God.

Already in 6:27 he had spoken of the Son of Man as going to give them the true bread in the future. Does this mean that all the statements about Jesus being the bread of life that follow refer only to his role after his death? This is highly unlikely and would sit very awkwardly in his story. Rather, it is as the one who, as the author put, came down from heaven that he gives life, namely, as the Word, the Son sent by the Father. The author is quite happy to say both: Jesus came and offered life and Jesus offers life also as the resurrected exalted one, the Son of Man. This is the golden thread running through John's Gospel.

These two different ways of speaking about Jesus may reflect the history of the chapter. Many see the statements in 6:51b–58 as something the author added to an earlier version of the chapter to highlight the link with Holy Communion. This is certainly possible, but we cannot know for sure.

What seems shocking to us, especially eating someone's flesh, needs to be heard within the context of the imagery of nourishment generally, which was widely used to speak of learning from someone's teaching, in that sense, feeding on them. That has been the focus throughout John 6. It was imagery used of God's Wisdom. As the book of Ben Sira puts it: "She will feed him with the bread of learning, and give him the water of wisdom to drink" (15:3). For John, Jesus is God's Wisdom and Word, and through him one finds the nourishment of eternal life. It is, therefore, Jesus, and ultimately God, who is the source of nourishment. The focus is not on what were probably elements of bread and wine or flesh and blood, but on these as a just another way of pointing to God's offer of eternal life.

The final section of this chapter deals with matters internal to the movement and probably reflects later divisions. Some, probably Jews, among the disciples felt the claims that came to be made about Jesus were going too far and so drop off from following him. In the setting of the story, the author places their departure during Jesus' life. The author then has Jesus again use Son of Man of himself, because he is referring to events linked to his death, namely his return to the Father and what follows: "What if you were to see the Son of Man going back up to where he was before?" (6:62). This is the contrast he has used before, in the conversations with Nathanael (1:50–51) and then with Nicodemus (3:13), saying that there is something even greater to come than his ministry on earth. It will be what is set in motion by the events surrounding his death.

By contrast to the dissenting disciples, the author has Peter declare on behalf of the twelve, referred to here for the first time, that he is "the holy one of God," recalling how Mark has him function as their spokesperson in first declaring, "You are the Messiah" (Mark 8:29). The two statements are variations of having Peter recognize Jesus as God's agent. The contrast between flesh and spirit in 6:63 is similar to the contrast between flesh and spirit and earthly and heavenly in John 3 in speaking of new birth and in John 4 when speaking of earthly temples. The long chapter ends with the foreboding reference to Judas' betrayal.

Reflection: What is the food that the author claims that Jesus brings?

Who Is This Fellow? (John 7:1—8:11)

Listening to John

7:1 After this Jesus was travelling around Galilee because he didn't want to do so in Judea because the Jews were looking for him to kill him. **2** Now the Jewish Festival of Booths was approaching **3** and his brothers said to him, "Move on from here and go to Judea, so that your disciples can see the deeds you're doing. **4** For no one does things in secret when seeking to be well known. If this is what you're on about, show yourself to the world." **5** For his brothers also did not believe in him.

6 Jesus said to them, "My time has not yet come; it's always your time. **7** The world can't hate you, but it hates me because I bear witness about it that its deeds are evil. **8** You, go up to the festival! I'll not go up to this festival, because it's not yet my time."

9 Having said this, he stayed in Galilee. **10** When his brothers had gone up to the festival, then he did go up; however, not openly, but secretly. **11** So the Jews were looking for him at the festival and were saying, "Where is the fellow?"

12 And there was a lot of arguing about him among the crowds. Some were saying, "He's a good chap." Others were saying, "No he's not; he's leading the mob astray." **13** No one however was speaking openly about him, for fear of the Jews.

14 When the festival was already halfway through, Jesus went into the temple and started teaching. **15** The Jews were surprised, saying, "How come he's sounding learned when he hasn't had an education?"

16 In response Jesus said to them, "My teaching is not mine but that of the one who sent me. **17** If anyone wants to do his will, he will recognize this teaching as coming from God rather than that I am speaking on my own authority. **18** People speaking on their own authority are looking for glory for themselves. The one who seeks glory from him who sent him is genuine and there's nothing phony about him. **19** Didn't Moses give you the Law? And none of you keeps the Law. Why then are you looking to kill me?"

²⁰ The crowd responded: "You've got a demon. Who's wanting to kill you?"

²¹ Jesus in reply said, "I have done one work, and you are all amazed. ²² Now think about this: Moses gave you the command to circumcise—though it wasn't really from Moses but from the fathers—and you circumcise a man on the Sabbath. ²³ Can't you see that a man will be circumcised on the Sabbath so as not to breach the Mosaic Law, but here you are having a go at me because I made a man whole on the Sabbath? ²⁴ Don't judge superficially, judge fairly when you judge!"

²⁵ Some of the Jerusalemites were saying, "This can't be the one they're wanting to kill, can it? ²⁶ 'Cos look, he's talking openly and they're not saying anything to him. Surely our leaders haven't come to recognize him as the Messiah, have they? ²⁷ We know about him, where he's from. When the Messiah comes, no one will know his origins."

²⁸ While teaching in the temple, Jesus therefore declared in a loud voice, "You know me, and you know where I'm from. I have not spoken of my own accord but the one who sent me is trustworthy, yet you don't know him; ²⁹ but I know him, because I came from him, and he sent me."

³⁰ They tried to get hold of him, but no one laid hands on him because his hour had not yet come. ³¹ Many in the crowd came to believe in him and were saying, "The Messiah, when he comes, will he do more miracles than he has done?"

³² The Pharisees heard the crowds discussing these things about him, and so the chief priests and the Pharisees sent their officers to arrest him. ³³ Jesus therefore commented, "I'll be with you for just a short time, and then I am going to the one who sent me. ³⁴ You'll look for me and won't find me. And where I'm going you can't come."

³⁵ The Jews in response discussed among themselves, "Where's he off to that we won't find him? Is he going to go to the Greek-speaking diaspora to teach the Greeks? ³⁶ What does his statement mean when he said: 'You'll look for me but not find me and where I am you won't be able to come'?"

³⁷ On the final day of the great festival Jesus stood up and with a loud voice declared, "If anyone thirsts let them come to me and let anyone who believes in me drink! ³⁸ As the Scripture has said, rivers of living water will flow from within him." ³⁹ He said this about the Spirit

which those who had come to believe in him would receive. For the Spirit had not yet been given, because Jesus had not yet been glorified.

⁴⁰ Some in the crowd who heard these words were saying, "Truly he is the prophet."

⁴¹ Others were saying, "He is the Messiah."

But some said, "Surely the Messiah won't hail from Galilee, will he? ⁴² For the Scripture said that when the Messiah comes, he'll be David's descendant and be from Bethlehem where David lived."

⁴³ And there was division in the crowd because of him. ⁴⁴ Some of them wanted to arrest him but no one laid hands on him. ⁴⁵ So the officers came to the chief priests and Pharisees, and they said to them, "Why didn't you arrest him?"

⁴⁶ The officers replied, "No one's ever spoken the way this fellow does."

⁴⁷ The Pharisees replied, "Have you been led astray, too? ⁴⁸ Surely, none of our leaders or of the Pharisees has believed in him, have they? ⁴⁹ But this crowd are simply ignorant of the Law, and they're accursed."

⁵⁰ Then Nicodemus, the one who came to him earlier, who was one of them, said to them, ⁵¹ "Surely our Law does not condemn a man without our first hearing from him and finding out what he's doing?"

⁵² In response they said to him, "You're not from Galilee, too, are you? Look and see: no prophet is to come from Galilee."

[*A later insertion:* ⁵³ Then they all went home. ⁸:¹ Jesus went to the Mount of Olives. ² The early next morning he went again into the temple and people came to him, and taking his seat he was teaching them. ³ The scribes and Pharisees brought a woman to him who had been caught committing adultery and stood her up in front of everyone ⁴ and said, "Teacher, this woman has been caught in the act of committing adultery. ⁵ In the Law, Moses instructed us to stone such perpetrators. What do you say?"

⁶ They were saying this to test him out, to be able to have something to accuse him of.

Jesus bent down and wrote with his finger on the ground. ⁷ When they kept on asking him, he stood up straight and said, "Let the person among you who is without sin be the first to throw a stone at her." ⁸ And again he bent down and wrote on the ground. ⁹ When they heard that they left one after another starting with the older ones, and he was left alone and the woman there with him. ¹⁰ Jesus stood up again and said to her, "Woman, where are they? Has no one condemned you?"

¹¹ She said, "No one, sir."

Jesus said, "Nor do I condemn you. Go, and from now on no more sinning!"]

Thinking About John

This chapter sees a shift to focus on opposition to Jesus among his fellow Jews. It begins with Jesus' family. His brothers suggest he go up to the Festival of Booths in Jerusalem. Why? To build his fan base among his disciples there. This is another variation on the theme of appropriate and inappropriate faith, which we found in 2:23–25, where Jesus did not believe in such believers, and the previous chapter where he had to escape from such believers who wanted to make him king (6:14–15). Fittingly, the author notes that his brothers, who clearly believed Jesus performed miracles, were not people of the kind of faith Jesus was looking for.

Can family get it wrong? According to John they certainly can. Mark has them share the concern that Jesus was mentally unstable and needed rescuing (3:20–21, 31–35), something Matthew and Luke chose to omit, probably because it did not sit well with the wondrous stories of Jesus' birth with which they opened their accounts of Jesus. John shows high regard for Mary, but the brothers? They fail to see.

Jesus told them he was not going to the festival, but then he does go. The author will not want us to see this as telling a lie. He connects it rather to the notion of the right time. Quite often he has Jesus say, now's not the right time. For Jesus the right time—or, as the author has him put it, the hour—is above all the hour of his death and all that his death inaugurates, his resurrection, exaltation, glorification, ascent to the Father, and what then flows from that. That moment, to start that final process, did come and so the author has Jesus go up after all, but secretly.

The focus of the passage then moves to what the crowds thought about Jesus. For knowing listeners to John's Gospel, the narrative has a touch of humor because they know the right answers to the crowd's ponderings. This is typical of the author's dramatic technique. They have heard how the Gospel began so they know the message: Jesus is the Word, God's Son, sent to be God's representative on earth offering God's gift of eternal life. This is the golden thread running through the Gospel. Uneducated? At the critics' level, yes! To people of faith, absolutely not, as the very Word and Wisdom of God! It is important to see that the author has Jesus emphasize that he is not acting independently of God but is totally obedient to his commission.

In 7:19–24 it comes as a surprise that we suddenly find Jesus responding to the criticism reported back in chapter 5 because he had healed a man on the Sabbath, especially since so much has happened in between time. Chapter 6 intervenes and that tells how he went back to Galilee in the interim. This has suggested to some that in an earlier form of the Gospel chapter 7 followed directly on from chapter 5. That would make sense, but it remains an intelligent guess. The passage itself has Jesus appeal for flexibility in handling Sabbath law. If you can circumcise people on the Sabbath, surely it's okay to heal them or make them whole—such is his argument, also with a touch of humor.

We then shift back to the drama of the crowd's ponderings about who Jesus might be. It continues with the seriously playful exchange about where Jesus was going. The listeners may smile again when they hear the Jews wonder if Jesus meant that he was going out into the wider Greek-speaking world, which they know is at one level nonsense, but at another level it is precisely what happens after Easter when, inspired by the Spirit, the disciples went far and wide into their world in mission.

It is, therefore, not so surprising that the author immediately has Jesus make the declaration that those believing in him would receive the Spirit and note that this would flow after Easter, after Jesus' glorification, his return to the Father. The imagery of water will have been suggested for the author by the daily morning ritual of fetching and pouring out water during the Festival of Booths.

The passage is slightly ambiguous, since it could refer to the Spirit flowing from within the believer or could mean it flows from Christ's body, as some suggest is symbolically depicted as what happens on the cross when Jesus is stabbed. The latter would fit the statements in the final discourses of Jesus with his disciples better, since here he talks about his giving the Spirit, but the statement would then have had to have made that clear. Were it to refer to Jesus, one would expect it to read "from within me." On balance, the words "as the Scripture has said, rivers of living water will flow from within him" are better taken as a reference to the believer.

No Scripture directly describes the Spirit flowing from within a person, but the allusion may be to Ezekiel with its image of water flowing out from the temple. The image with which Jesus' statement begins, of drinking as opening oneself to God's goodness, was well known, and perhaps best represented in the book of Isaiah:

> Ho, everyone who thirsts, come to the waters; and you that have no money, come, buy and eat! Come, buy wine and milk without money and without price. (Isa 55:1)

Jesus' declaration in 7:37–39, therefore, has a dual focus: drinking of the water of life offered by Jesus in his person already during his ministry (as in John 6:35 and John 4) and the promise of the Spirit after Easter inspiring and empowering people for mission. We find a similar dual focus in John 6, which depicts Jesus as offering the bread of life during his ministry and also as pointing ahead to receiving life through eating his flesh and drinking his blood—rather stark imagery of Holy Communion. In pointing forward to what it would mean to be a disciple after Easter, John embraces the notion that it would be from within the believer that the fruit of the Spirit would be born, love flowing from within, rather than love as a command to be fulfilled as an external requirement.

We return in 7:40 to ponderings about who Jesus is, but this time with the threat overhanging the conversation of Jesus' possible arrest. It includes some views that circulated at the time, such as that the Messiah would appear incognito and would have to be a descendant of David. The author's drama assumes that his listeners do know that Jesus was indeed a descendant of David and was born in Bethlehem, data we know from Matthew and Luke's birth narratives, and perhaps also their source. Well may the readers smile as the narrative proceeds. They know much more.

Here we meet for the first time official Jewish intervention out of concern about Jesus and his actions. The author has Nicodemus plead for a fair hearing. Some listeners would remember Jesus' conversation where at his level of understanding Nicodemus had declared Jesus to be a teacher come from God. The earlier verses in this chapter had also spoken of Jesus as a teacher but in a more profound sense. That, too, might make a connection for them with Nicodemus, who will reappear with Joseph of Arimathea after Jesus' death as a secret disciple (19:38–40).

At the end of chapter 7 we are left with Jesus under threat. In that sense, his time, the hour, has come and the chapters that follow will heighten the sense of danger finally leading to Jesus' crucifixion. This means that the author pictures Jesus as active in the general area of Judea for another six months before his demise, the Festival of Booths being normally in October and the Passover in April. Mark's account has Jesus enter Judea in Mark 10, but gives no indication of a long stay, perhaps more realistic historically given the danger he would have been in.

Between John 7:52 and 8:11, some later manuscripts include a passage that may well have been a story that once circulated independently and was inserted here. The best and oldest manuscripts do not contain it. It was almost certainly not originally part of the Fourth Gospel but may nevertheless preserve early and perhaps even historical memory. Jesus is confronted with the case of a woman caught in adultery. He is faced with a trap. Does he follow biblical law and have her stoned or respect Roman law, which forbad such executions? His clever response was to turn on his accusers and suggest provocatively that those without sin should throw the first stone. None did, and she was sent off with the challenge not to sin anymore. The man involved is not mentioned, probably reflecting the trend still current to blame women. It does depict Jesus as acting out of compassion, while cleverly escaping being trapped.

John 8 continues the exchange at the Festival of Booths but moves more directly to dealing with conflict and rejection.

Reflection: What is the hour to which the author has Jesus refer and what significance does it have according to this passage?

The Devil's Children! (John 8:12–59)

Listening to John

8:12 Again Jesus spoke to them saying, "I am the light of the world. Whoever follows me won't be walking in darkness but will have the light of life."

13 The Pharisees said to him, "You are testifying on your own behalf. Your testimony doesn't stack up."

14 In response Jesus told them, "If I testify on my own behalf, my testimony is true, because I know where I came from and where I'm going, but you don't know where I'm from or where I'm going. **15** You judge at the level of the flesh; I don't judge anyone. **16** And if I judge, my judgment is trustworthy, because I'm not on my own, for there's me and the Father who sent me. **17** It is written in your law that the evidence of two or three witnesses is trustworthy. **18** I testify on my own behalf and my Father testifies on my behalf."

19 They started to say to him, "Where is your Father?"

Jesus answered, "You know neither me nor my Father. If you had known me, you would have known my Father."

20 He said these words by the treasury in the temple and no one arrested him, because his hour had not yet come. **21** So he said to them again, "I am going away, and you will look for me, and you will die in your sin. Where I am going you cannot come."

22 The Jews said, "He's not going to kill himself, is he, that he's saying, 'where I am going you can't come'?"

23 And he said to them, "You are from below; I am from above. You are of this world; I am not of this world. **24** So I told you that you will die in your sins."

25 So they said to him, "Who are you?"

Jesus said to them, "What I said from the start, in talking to you. **26** I have lots to say and judge about you, but the one who sent me is trustworthy and the things I hear from him I declare to the world."

⁲⁷ They didn't know that he was speaking to them about the Father. ²⁸ So Jesus told them, "When you have lifted up the Son of Man, then you will know that I'm the one and that I do nothing of my own accord but declare the things the Father has taught me. ²⁹ And the one who sent me is with me and does not leave me alone, because I always do what is pleasing to him."

³⁰ While he was saying all this, many came to believe in him. ³¹ So Jesus said to the Jews who had come to believe in him, "If you stick with my message, you are my disciples ³² and you will know the truth and the truth will set you free."

³³ They answered him, "We are the seed of Abraham and have never been enslaved to anyone. How come you are saying, 'You'll become free'?"

³⁴ Jesus replied to them, "Truly, truly, I tell you, anyone who does sin is a slave of sin. ³⁵ The slave does not stay in the household forever, but the Son remains forever. ³⁶ If the Son liberates you, you will be really free. ³⁷ I know you are Abraham's seed, but you are wanting to kill me, because my message has found no place in you. ³⁸ What I have seen with the Father I speak about, and you do what you have seen with your father."

³⁹ They said in response, "Our father is Abraham."

Jesus said to them, "If you were children of Abraham, you would do the deeds of Abraham, ⁴⁰ but now you are wanting to kill a man who has spoken the truth to you which I heard from God. This is something Abraham would never have done. ⁴¹ You are doing the deeds of your father."

They said to him, "We are not bastards, but have one Father, namely God."

⁴² Jesus said to them, "If God were your father, you would love me because I came from God and am here now. I haven't come off my own bat, but he sent me. ⁴³ Why don't you recognize what I'm talking about? Because you can't accept my message. ⁴⁴ You are children of your father the devil, and you want to do what he desires. He was a murderer from the beginning and lacked integrity because there's no integrity in him. When he tells lies, he is speaking from his being, because he is a liar and the father of lies. ⁴⁵ I tell you the truth, and you do not believe me. ⁴⁶ Who among you is going to charge me with sin?

I speak the truth. Why don't you believe me? ⁴⁷ The one who is born of God speaks the message of God. You know why you don't listen? It's because you are not children of God."

⁴⁸ The Jews then responded saying, "Aren't we right in saying you're a Samaritan and demon possessed?"

⁴⁹ Jesus answered, "I'm not demon possessed, but honor my Father and you dishonor me. ⁵⁰ I'm not looking for glory for myself. There is one who seeks it and assesses. ⁵¹ Truly, truly, I tell you, if you stick with my message, you will never see death."

⁵² The Jews said to him, "Now we know you're demon possessed. Abraham died as did the prophets and you're saying, if anyone sticks with your message, they'll never taste death. ⁵³ Are you greater than our father Abraham, who died? And the prophets? What are making yourself out to be?"

⁵⁴ Jesus responded, "If I glorify myself, my glory is nothing. My Father is the one glorifying me, who you say is your God. ⁵⁵ And you don't know him, but I know him. If I were to say I don't know him, I would be like you, a liar. But I do know him, and I stick with his message. ⁵⁶ Abraham your father rejoiced to see my day and saw it and was glad."

⁵⁷ So the Jews said to him, "You aren't yet fifty years old, and you've seen Abraham?"

⁵⁸ Jesus told them, "Truly, truly, I tell you, before Abraham came into being, I existed."

⁵⁹ They picked up stones to throw at him, but Jesus slipped away and left the temple.

Thinking About John

It might come as a surprise that suddenly Jesus speaks of himself as the light of the world, until we realize that the author is playing with the daily evening ritual of the Festival of Booths. It entailed lighting candles. This is yet another of the author's creative depictions of Jesus after saying he gives the water of life and depicting him as the bread of life.

In this chapter we are dealing with further variations on the theme of who the author depicts Jesus to be, namely the Son sent from the Father to offer life. Its focus is debate and disagreement, very probably reflecting disagreements between the author's community and members of the synagogues who rejected their message. The language and concepts do not reflect what we know of the historical Jesus from elsewhere, so they have more to do with that conflict than with history.

The Pharisees challenge the claim that the author has Jesus make of himself. A debate then ensues in which Jesus simply asserts his authority as the one sent from God. He accuses his critics of failing to accept this because they are thinking superficially, that is, at the level of the earthly rather than the heavenly. The author has Jesus support his claim to be providing reliable evidence by appealing to the biblical rule that where two or three witnesses agree in giving testimony it is reliable, but then cites himself and God as the two witnesses, not a very convincing argument.

There is typical playfulness in the way the author has composed the dialogue. His two witnesses are Jesus himself and his Father, but, of course, they think he's talking about his human father. Laugh! Similarly, there is an element of dramatic irony in the way the author then has Jesus say he is going away. Listeners to the Gospel know he means his return through death to God, but the author has the critics wonder where he is going and wonder if he is going to commit suicide. Laugh again! Seriously—because he will, in fact, die. Listeners would have understood the deeper truth behind the allusion.

The division is sharp, and the author has Jesus declare that his critics are to die in their sins. As the critics question Jesus, asking who he thinks he is, the listeners to the Gospel are by now well informed to be able to answer. Again, we find the author saying that there is more, and using the title Son of Man to describe it, just as in 1:51, 3:13; and 6:62. This greater event to come is his death and what that inaugurates. Again, the author plays with double meaning to describe it and has Jesus speak about being lifted up, which unfaith would see as crucifixion, but faith saw as his being lifted up by God to heaven! Then, they will or could come to appreciate who he really is. Who is he? The author keeps having Jesus repeat the claim that he has come as the Son sent by the Father.

In 8:30 the author introduces Jews who did come to believe Jesus' message and has Jesus challenge them to stick with it. What seemed like progress reverses into an argument when the author has Jesus claim that they would be liberated from slavery, something to which they object. This then starts a downhill slide into accusation and counter accusation.

He rejects their claim to be children of Abraham and instead declares them children of the devil. Taken out of its original context of intra-Jewish debate, this fitted well into the anti-Semitism of the times and then of later centuries, which generated hatred towards Jews in general and inspired some of history's worst moments, such as the gassing of six million Jews in the Holocaust.

The author has this awful exchange go further, with the critics declaring Jesus demon possessed, in other words, off his head, mad. It sounded mad for someone to claim he could make people live forever and even madder to claim that he was in existence before Abraham. The listeners will have understood what Jesus was saying in quite different ways, especially if the opening verses of the Gospel were still in their memory, because then, of course, on that basis he was in the beginning with God, so in existence before Abraham.

There is no real dialogue here. Instead, the author depicts the conflict as deadly. The critics are not just wrong not to believe Jesus. They are bad, children of the devil. There is no middle ground. We can only imagine what it must have been like to have your message rejected. It split families. It split communities. There would be hurt and anger.

One way to deal with it might have been to enter dialogue, but at times it would have simply degenerated into personal accusation such as we see here. Denigrating those who dissent from us is far from loving one's enemies. In this chapter the author reflects such alienation and anger. We need therefore to read it with minds informed by the way of love and respect, and so not uncritically.

Reflection: What dangers do you see in the author's composition?

Who's Really Blind? (John 9:1–41)

Listening to John

9:1 As he was going along, he saw a man blind from birth. **2** And his disciples asked him, "Rabbi, who sinned, this man or his parents that he was born blind?"

3 Jesus replied, "Neither he nor his parents sinned, but it is for the purpose of highlighting God's actions in healing him. **4** We must do the deeds of the one who sent me while it is day, because night is coming when no one can do them. **5** As long as I am in the world, I am the light of the world."

6 Having said this, he spat on the ground and made some mud with his saliva and applied the mud to the man's eyes **7** and told him, "Go and wash in the pool of Siloam" (which translated means "sent one"). So he went off and washed and came back able to see.

8 His neighbors and those who had seen him prior to this as a beggar started to say, "Isn't this the guy who was sitting and begging?"

9 Some were saying, "It's him," and others, "No, it just looks like him."

He himself said, "It is me!"

10 They said to him, "How were your eyes given sight?"

11 He replied, "The man called Jesus made some mud and applied it to my eyes and told me, 'Go to Siloam and wash yourself.' So I went and washed myself and now I can see."

12 And they said to him, "Where is this fellow?"

He said, "I don't know."

13 They took him to the Pharisees, the man once blind. **14** Now the day that Jesus made the mud and opened his eyes was a Sabbath. **15** So the Pharisees, too, started asking him again how he got his sight back, and he told then, "He put mud on my eyes, and I washed, and now I can see."

16 Some of the Pharisees said, "This fellow can't be from God, because he doesn't keep the Sabbath."

Others were commenting, "But how can someone who's a sinner do such miracles?"

And they were divided in their views.

[17] So they said to the blind man again, "What do you say about him for opening your eyes?"

He said, "He's a prophet."

[18] The Jews didn't believe the story about him, that he was blind and was enabled to see, until they called the parents of the man who had recovered his sight, [19] and asked them, "Is this your son, that you say was born blind? How come he's now able to see?"

[20] In response his parents said, "We know this is our son and that he was born blind, [21] but how come he can now see we have no idea. Ask him. He's old enough; he can speak for himself."

[22] The parents said this because they were afraid of the Jews, because the Jews had already reached an agreement that anyone confessing him to be the Messiah was to be banned from the synagogue. [23] That's why his parents said, "He's old enough, ask him." [24] So they called the man who was blind a second time and said to him, "Give glory to God. We know that this fellow is a sinner."

[25] He replied, "I don't know if he's a sinner; all I know is that once I was blind and now, I can see."

[26] They therefore said to him, "What did he do to you? How did he give you your sight?"

[27] He answered them, "I told you already, and you didn't listen. Why do you want to hear it again? Do you, too, want to become his disciples?"

[28] But they abused him and said, "You are a disciple of that fellow, but we are disciples of Moses. [29] We know that God spoke to Moses, but as for this fellow we don't know where he hails from."

[30] The man responded and told them, "This is amazing. You don't know where he hails from, and yet he was able to give me my sight. [31] We know that God doesn't listen to sinners, but if anyone honors God and does his will, he listens to them. [32] Never has it been heard that someone gave sight to a man born blind. [33] If he weren't from God, he wouldn't have been able to do anything."

[34] In reply they told him, "You were totally born in sin, and you really think you can teach us?" And they sent him packing.

³⁵ Now Jesus heard that they had sent him packing, so finding him, said, "Do you believe in the Son of Man?"

³⁶ He responded, saying, "Who is he, sir, so that I can believe in him?"

³⁷ Jesus told him, "You've actually seen him; it's the one speaking with you."

³⁸ He said, "I believe, sir," and knelt down in front of him.

³⁹ And Jesus said, "For judgment I came into this world, so that those not seeing may come to see and those seeing might become blind."

⁴⁰ Some Pharisees who were with him heard this and said to him, "Are we blind, too?"

⁴¹ Jesus told them, "If you were blind, you would have no guilt. But now that you are saying we see, your guilt remains."

Thinking About John

This is a wonderful example of the author's dramatic skill. It starts with the disciples pondering whether a blind man's blindness is the product of his parents' guilt or his own and ends by talking about a different kind of guilt and blindness, the blindness of those who have sight but do not see who Jesus is. This is a confronting episode with allusions to what some of John's listeners may well have experienced in their own conflicts with Jews, in many instances, probably fellow Jews.

The author plays with imagery of light and darkness, which fits well with blindness and sight. In the previous chapter he had used the light imagery of the daily lighting of evening candles during the Festival of Booths, to have Jesus declare, "I am the light of the world," and so repeats it here. To see in Jesus the light, ultimately the light of God, is truly to see. Not to believe is to be blind, to be in darkness. Those are the parameters.

To develop the drama the author uses a healing story, which may well go back a long time, even to the historical Jesus. For some, the story will recall the healing of Naaman, the Syrian, who was also told to wash and be healed (2 Kings 5). People used to believe that human saliva had healing qualities and we see that primitive medicine reflected in this story. We see it also used in the story Mark brings in 8:22–26, which depicts Jesus using saliva on a blind man. Whatever the story's origin, the author clearly saw it as fitting to have it follow the conflicts depicted in the previous chapter. The link with the pool of Siloam in Jerusalem may be part of the tradition, but the author plays with the name, which conveniently means "Sent One," referring to the man, but in a sense also supremely to Jesus himself.

Linking illness to guilt was an assumption many shared and is illustrated in Mark 2:1–12 where Mark portrays Jesus as healing the man let down through the roof by declaring his sins forgiven. Here in John 9 the assumption of guilt is rejected, albeit in favor of seeing the blindness by implication as part of a divine plan, also not always a helpful explanation. All too often people feel or are made to feel guilty about illness or disability and we now know that these have multiple causes, even if occasionally people may do things that bring harm to themselves. Mostly it is not so.

The play with guilt, as already noted, is part of the drama, which has the Pharisees portrayed as guilty and blind. It is almost entertaining, at least in a serious kind of way that would engage listeners, the manner in which the author narrates the exchanges with onlookers, then with Pharisees, then with the man's parents, and finally with the man himself. Already the play about night coming points to what they know will come: Jesus' death.

The exchange with the Pharisees takes off from the fact that the healing took place on the Sabbath and entailed work, making mud. Locating it on a Sabbath may be the author's addition for the drama. It is meant to be heard as absurd that they are putting strict Sabbath observance ahead of healing the man of his blindness. Such commonsense disapproval can also be found in Mark's controversy stories and already in John 5, where it also seemed added as the detail that sets off the drama there. How unreasonable to complain about someone being restored to health! Such is the intended response.

The exchange between the parents and "the Jews" includes reference to the fear of being banned from the synagogue (9:22), a danger to which Jesus points in his final speeches (16:2) and is mentioned in 12:42. This is likely to have been something some among John's listeners had experienced when it became no longer acceptable to claim that Jesus was the Messiah. Eventually the blind man is also turfed out (9:34), also a reminder of the painful experience that John and his communities will have had to process.

The final exchange between the Jews and the man recalls many of the author's strategies. When he has the Jews say, "we don't know where he hails from" (9:30), the listeners might well smile. They know he comes from above, a standard theme of the author. The contrast with Moses we have met before. The author reframes Moses and the Scriptures to be witnesses to who Jesus is, not to be set in contrast to him. Their statement that the man was born in sin is an attempt to explain why he was blind from birth, something the author has already had Jesus reject.

When the author has Jesus refer in this context to himself as the Son of Man, this might come as a surprise until we see what follows. For there Jesus speaks of himself fulfilling the role attributed in tradition to the Son of Man, as already mentioned in 5:27, namely the exercise of judgment. Here the author depicts it as taking place in the present as people are confronted with who Jesus is and either accept and believe or do not. Those who do not are the real blind people.

John was not the first to use blindness and sight metaphorically. Mark does so to great effect in Mark 8–10 in depicting the disciples as blind to the values of Jesus and putting such observations alongside stories of Jesus' healing the blind at Bethesda and blind Bartimaeus. The author's focus is not fellow believers, but those Jews who did not accept the claims about Jesus being made by him and his community. The seriously playful drama in John 9 serves in part to help them process that rejection. Its positive statements focus on the light. Its negative statements, like those in the previous chapter, denigrate dissent in ways that build potential for unhealthy trends.

Reflection: What is really being said with the imagery of light?

3

Facing Rejection

The Good Shepherd and His Sheep (John 10:1–42)

Listening to John

¹⁰:¹ "Truly, truly, I tell you, anyone not coming into the sheepyard through the gate but getting up into it another way, that person is a thief and a sheep stealer. ² But the one who enters via the gate is the shepherd of the sheep. ³ The gatekeeper opens the gate for him, and the sheep listen to his voice, and he calls his own sheep by name, and he leads them out. ⁴ Whenever he leads all his own out, he goes ahead of them, and the sheep follow him because they recognize his voice. ⁵ In no way will they follow a stranger, but will run away from him, because they don't recognize the voice of strangers."

⁶ Jesus told them this parable, but they didn't realize what it was that he was talking to them about. ⁷ Again Jesus said, "Truly, truly, I tell you, I am the gate for the sheep. ⁸ All who came before me are thieves and sheep stealers, but the sheep didn't listen to them. ⁹ I am the gate. If any enters via me, they will be safe and will come and go and find pasture. ¹⁰ The thief comes just to steal and kill and destroy. I came so that they might have life and have it abundantly.

¹¹ I am the good shepherd. The good shepherd lays down his life for the sheep. ¹² A temporary employee who isn't the shepherd, who doesn't own the sheep, when he sees the wolf coming, will abandon the sheep and go for his life—and the wolf will grab them and send them

scattering—¹³ because he's a short-term employee and doesn't really care about the sheep.

¹⁴ I am the good shepherd, and I know my own, and my own know me. ¹⁵ As my Father knows me, so I know the Father, and I lay down my life for the sheep. ¹⁶ I've got other sheep who are not in this yard, and I need to be rounding them up too, and they will listen to my voice, and they'll become one flock with one shepherd. ¹⁷ This is why the Father loves me, because I lay down my life so that I can take it up again. ¹⁸ No one takes it from me, but I lay it down of my own accord. I have the right to lay it down, and I have the right to take it up again. I received this mandate from my Father."

¹⁹ There was a division among the Jews because of these words. ²⁰ Many of them were saying, "He's got a demon, and he's lost his mind. Why listen to him?"

²¹ Others were saying, "These aren't the words of someone possessed of a demon. Surely a demon wouldn't be able to give sight to the blind."

²² The Festival of Dedication was on at that time, and it was winter. ²³ And Jesus was taking a walk in the temple in Solomon's portico. ²⁴ So the Jews gathered around him and said to him, "How long are you going to hold us in suspense? If you are the Messiah, tell us openly."

²⁵ Jesus responded, "I told you, and you didn't believe me. The works that I do in my Father's name, they are my evidence, ²⁶ but you don't believe, because you are not my sheep. ²⁷ My sheep listen to my voice, and I know them, and they follow me, ²⁸ and I grant them eternal life, and they won't ever perish, and no one will snatch them out of my hand. ²⁹ What my Father has given me is worth more than anything, and no one can snatch them out of the Father's hands. ³⁰ I and my Father are at one."

³¹ Again the Jews picked up rocks to stone him with.

³² Jesus responded, "I have shown you many good deeds done on my Father's behalf. What kind of deed are you going to stone me for?"

³³ The Jews replied, "We're not going to stone you because of a good deed, but because of blasphemy and because you, a human being, are making yourself out to be God."

³⁴ Jesus answered, "Haven't you read what is written in the Law, 'I tell you, you are gods'? ³⁵ If they called people gods to whom God's

word came—and the Scripture can't be set aside—³⁶ are you really then saying of the one whom God sanctified and sent into the world, 'You're blaspheming,' because I said I am God's Son? ³⁷ If I'm not doing the works of my Father, don't believe in me. ³⁸ But if I am doing them, if you won't believe in me, at least believe in the works, so that you can realize and know that the Father is in me and I am in the Father."

³⁹ Again they tried to arrest him, but he escaped from their hands. ⁴⁰ And he went off again to the other side of the Jordan to the place where John was first baptizing and stayed there. ⁴¹ And many came to him and said, "John did no miracle, but everything John said about this man is true." ⁴² And many came to believe in him there.

Thinking About John

No sheep dogs and motorbikes, this is the ancient world where the shepherd walked in front of the sheep, and they followed because the shepherd often fed them extra food. The sheep followed the shepherd, and the shepherd would then lead them to the safety of a sheepyard overnight to protect them from wild animals and lead them out again in the morning when it was light.

Shepherds from the ancient world have been a rich source of imagery down through the centuries, though often reduced to romantic pictures, such as of Jesus with cuddly lambs. In part this is because we have taken the Latin word for shepherd, *pastor*, into our language and so usually seen shepherd as a pastoral image in the metaphorical sense of pastoral care. In their world it was more often a political image used of leaders, as far back as the Pharaohs of Egypt. Shepherd was a common image for a king or ruler. Rulers should be like shepherds and take into account the welfare of their subjects, a value as relevant now when applied to politicians as it ever was.

How does the author have Jesus use it? Clearly with a critical edge to begin with, contrasting Jesus with others. We might ask: Who, then, are these others? Clearly other would-be leaders. Does this reflect conflict among leaders of local congregations? This is unlikely. The broader context is processing rejection by Jews, and for many that would have been fellow Jews, but it might also refer to wider conflicts within the Jesus movement. Whether still current or reflecting past history, it is very probably a barbed response to those who in the past sought to persuade or control would-be followers of Jesus.

Again, as in previous chapters, we are, therefore, in the arena of conflict and demarcation. The author offers listeners facing such conflict the comfort of believing that they are the ones God has given to Jesus as his sheep and the others are not, a comfort to insiders about themselves and a kind of false comfort about why others had not joined them. It is the exclusive language we have met before, which sounds like a closed system. If God determines that some reject the gospel, then they surely are not to be blamed. They are "meant" to reject. But that is not how the language works. They are blameworthy in their rejection and language like this might persuade them to join us. It is not a closed system, and if it is read as such it can become a dangerous concept.

The author plays with the imagery. Initially, he contrasts Jesus with those wanting to steal the sheep, then uses the image of Jesus as the gateway, and then returns to Jesus as the shepherd, the good shepherd in contrast to others. The image works well. Personal contact with the sheep, including recognizing the shepherd's voice, was important. It made sense also to point out that someone just filling in in the role would not have the motivation to stick with the sheep and defend them. The genuine shepherd would put his life on the line to protect his sheep.

While making his case for the special relationship between Jesus as shepherd and his sheep, the author plays further with the image by having Jesus intimate that there were sheep elsewhere who would also become part of his one flock. The reference is to the wider mission, including the gentile mission, and so would be a way at hinting at the inclusion of at least some of the author's listeners.

The notion of a shepherd laying down his life for the sheep is slightly awkward. A shepherd should make every effort to keep himself alive to protect them. He's not much use to them if he's dead! But this is imagery. The author wants to point to Jesus' willingness to put his life on the line. In the author's account, Jesus' death plays multiple roles, not only the traditional notion of being like a sacrifice, present though not prominent in his account, but also the notion that it would be the start of an event that would include his resurrection, return to the Father, and the setting off of the great expansion of his message to all the world. He will later have Jesus refer to this expansion as the greater works than what he himself had done (14:12). This makes sense of his statement, "I lay down my life so that I can take it up again" (10:17). Taking it up again, he will send the Spirit to initiate that expansion.

In 10:19–24, John depicts those listening to Jesus' statements as not quite knowing what to make of him and alluding back to the healing reported in John 9. As in previous chapters, the author has Jesus appeal to his actions as evidence of who he is and will have evoked smiles from his listeners when the interlocutors want Jesus to tell them whether he is the Messiah. Of course he is!

It is at this point that the author has Jesus return to the sheep and shepherd imagery (10:27–29), initially to repeat the highly problematic explanation that the failure of some to believe is because they have not been chosen to be Jesus' sheep, and then to offer the assurance that those who are his sheep will be cared for by him and God, reassurance for his listeners. It is in this context of having Jesus speak of his and of God's assured protection that the author then has Jesus declare "I and my Father are at one," literally, "I and the Father are one" (10:30). It does not mean the two are equated as though the author is saying, Jesus is the Father and the Father is Jesus. It is rather a statement of oneness in the sense that Jesus is totally at one with what God wants and so can act on God's behalf.

It did however sound like it was a claim to be God, as the author has the unbelieving Jews claim (10:33). The author has Jesus then defend himself by citing Psalm 82, "I say, 'You are gods, children of the Most High, all of you'" (82:6). The Psalms were sometimes classified broadly as "the Law," as belonging to Scripture. As an argument, citing this statement from the psalm hardly addresses the real issue, because the author is claiming much more about Jesus than what this psalm assumes. The real issue, which citing the psalm does not address, was how Jesus as a human being could claim to be God's Son, the one who was with God from the beginning, was God, but was with God, and therefore God in a different sense.

The language of being in another person, as in the statement, "The Father is in me and I am in the Father" (10:38), which will reappear again in John's narrative of Jesus' last words to his disciples, expresses intimate connection. It will be used also of believers being in Christ and Christ in them. It expresses, however, a limited mutuality between two persons who are not in fact equal. The author often has Jesus speak of being sent and doing his Father's will, but never the reverse, his sending the Father and Father doing his will. Such language lent itself to being misunderstood as blasphemy, but also left later generations with the task of trying to explain it, resulting in the Christian creeds.

In the time well before the creeds sought to hold it all together, the author was depicting an encounter with Jesus as God's agent, and embodying God's Wisdom and Word, as in effect an encounter with God without saying Jesus was God or a god. The result of his efforts was both to elevate Jesus to a godlike position and at the same time reduce him to being more like a window.

The author was ultimately portraying Jesus as advocating for God. God is central, and all the language about sonship, being sent as an envoy, and doing God's works were ways ultimately of portraying Jesus as presenting God as the source of life and hope, represented in the images of water, bread, light. This is the golden thread running through this Gospel. In that sense he was the gate, the way, and the shepherd, who leads the way to the Father, and, as the author insists, exclusively so. Others would want to affirm that God is indeed life and hope and claim that any way that genuinely leads there and not elsewhere is to be recognized as the way. For followers of Jesus that would then be recognized as consistent and coherent with the way Jesus represented it.

Reflection: How does the imagery of shepherd help in understanding the author's portrait of Jesus?

The Resurrection and the Life (John 11:1–57)

Listening to John

^{11:1} Now there was a man who was ill, Lazarus from Bethany, the village of Mary and Martha, her sister. ² It was Mary who had anointed the Lord with myrrh and wiped his feet with her hair, whose brother Lazarus was ill. ³ So the sisters sent for Jesus saying, "Lord, your friend is ill."

⁴ When Jesus heard it, he said, "This illness won't lead to death but is for God's glory, so that the Son of God may be glorified through it."

⁵ Now Jesus was fond of Martha and her sister and Lazarus. ⁶ So when he heard that he was ill, he stayed where he was for a couple of days. ⁷ Then after that he told his disciples, "Let's go to Judea again."

⁸ His disciples said to him, "Rabbi, the Jews are currently looking for you to stone you, and you really want to go there?"

⁹ Jesus answered, "Aren't there twelve hours in the day? If anyone walks around during daytime, they won't trip up, because they see the light of this world. ¹⁰ But if anyone walks around at night, they'll trip up, because they've got no light."

¹¹ He said this to them and then later, afterwards, told them, "Lazarus our friend has fallen asleep, but I'll go and wake him up."

¹² His disciples said to him, "Lord, if he's gone to sleep, he will be safe."

¹³ Jesus had spoken about his death, but they thought he was talking about his resting asleep. ¹⁴ So Jesus therefore stately plainly, "Lazarus has died. ¹⁵ And I'm glad for your sake that I was not there, so that you will believe, but let's go to him."

¹⁶ So Thomas, called The Twin, said to his fellow disciples, "Let's go that we might die along with him."

¹⁷ When Jesus arrived, he found he'd been already four days in the tomb. ¹⁸ Bethany was near Jerusalem, about fifteen stadia [two miles; five kilometers] away. ¹⁹ Many Jews had come to Martha and Mary to

comfort them because of their brother. [20] So Martha, when she heard that Jesus was coming, went and met him, while Mary stayed sitting at home. [21] Martha said to Jesus, "Lord, if you'd been here, my brother wouldn't have died, [22] but I now know that whatever you ask of God, God will do for you."

[23] Jesus told her, "Lazarus your brother will rise."

[24] Martha said to him, "I know that he will rise at the resurrection on the last day."

[25] Jesus said to her, "I am the resurrection and the life. Anyone believing in me even if they die will live, [26] and all who live and believe in me will never die. Do you believe this?"

[27] She said to him, "Yes, Lord, I have the firm faith that you are the Messiah, the Son of God, the one meant to come into the world."

[28] And having said that, she went off and summoned Mary her sister, telling her privately, "The teacher's here and is calling for you."

[29] When she heard, she got up quickly and went to him.

[30] Jesus had not yet entered the village but was where Martha had encountered him. [31] The Jews who were with her in her home offering her comfort saw that Mary got up quickly and headed out, and they followed her, thinking that she was going to the tomb to weep there. [32] So Mary came to where Jesus was and seeing him, she fell down at his feet, saying to him, "Lord, if you'd been here, my brother wouldn't have died."

[33] So when Jesus saw her weeping and the Jews who had come with her weeping, he was moved inside and disturbed.

[34] And he said, "Where have you put him?"

They said to him, "Lord, come and see!"

[35] Jesus wept.

[36] So the Jews said, "See how much he loved him."

[37] Some of them said, "This fellow opened the eyes of a blind man, couldn't he have prevented this man from dying?"

[38] Jesus, again deeply moved, arrived at the tomb. It was a cave with a rock blocking it shut. [39] Jesus said, "Take the rock away."

Martha, the dead man's sister, said, "Lord, it'll smell; he's been there for four days."

[40] Jesus said to her, "Didn't I tell you you'd see God's glory if you believed?

⁴¹ So they took the rock away. Then Jesus lifted up his eyes and said, "Father, I thank you that you hear me. ⁴² I knew that you always hear me, but for the sake of the crowd standing here I've said this, so that they may believe that you sent me." ⁴³ And having said that, he cried out with a loud voice, "Lazarus, come on out!"

⁴⁴ The dead man came out with his feet and hands bound in strips of cloth and his face covered with cloth. And Jesus told them, "Release him and set him free to move."

⁴⁵ So, many of the Jews who had come to Mary, when they saw what he had done, came to believe in him. ⁴⁶ Some of them went off to the Pharisees and told them what Jesus had done. ⁴⁷ The chief priests and the Pharisees therefore got together and said, "What are we going to do, because this fellow is performing many miracles? ⁴⁸ If we let him carry on like this, everyone will believe in him, and the Romans will come and do away with both this place and our people."

⁴⁹ Then one of them, namely Caiaphas, the high priest that year, said to them, "You're pretty dumb. ⁵⁰ Don't you realize that it's fitting to have one person die on behalf of the people to make sure the whole nation won't be destroyed?" ⁵¹ He didn't say this of his own accord, but as the high priest that year he was making a prophetic statement, namely that Jesus was going to die for the nation, ⁵² and not just for the nation but so that all God's children scattered abroad might be gathered into one. ⁵³ So from that moment they resolved to kill him.

⁵⁴ Therefore Jesus no longer wandered openly among the Jews but left there for the countryside close to the desert, reaching the village called Ephraim, and stayed there with his disciples.

⁵⁵ The Passover of the Jews was approaching, and many were making their way to Jerusalem from the countryside before Passover to purify themselves. ⁵⁶ They were looking for Jesus and conversed with one another as they stood around in the temple wondering, "What do you think? He's surely not going to come for the festival, is he?"

⁵⁷ The chief priests and the Pharisees had given instructions that if anyone knew where he was, they should make it known, so that they could arrest him.

Thinking About John

This is another of John's dramas, again somewhat playful but seriously so. The author employs ambiguous meanings of words to enhance the drama. To fall asleep was a way of talking about dying, as we, today, will say someone passed away, meaning they died. "If he's gone to sleep, he will be safe" uses a word, here translated "safe," which can also have the meaning "be saved"—another word play.

Being raised and being resurrected is also at play in the narrative. Lazarus is resuscitated and will die again, who knows when, days, months, or years later. This is not the same as resurrection on the last day, which entails a new form of existence. Even beyond that, the author has Jesus declare himself to be resurrection and life, elevating the listeners' attention above the literal story, because Lazarus would eventually die, whereas Jesus' claim was that people would never die, meaning something at a spiritual level and is implying that those who come to faith in him have already experienced resurrection. The key statement the author has Jesus make, "I am the resurrection and the life," treats the story of what is in effect a temporary resuscitation symbolically, leaving it behind to talk of something quite different: eternal life now and beyond death. This is typical of the way the author shifts the focus from the fantastic miracle to deeper meaning, as he did in the healing of the blind man and the feeding of the five thousand, and as intimated in his earlier challenge to Nicodemus and others stuck at the level of miracles as propaganda (2:23—3:5).

The author employs double meaning also in having the high priest declare that it was appropriate that Jesus die for the sake of the nation. He meant it literally, but the author takes it in a more profound sense and explains this against the background that in their year of office high priests could allegedly (and unwittingly!) make inspired utterances. This reflects the fact that the author is beholden to traditions that held the cult in high regard.

The author assumes in 11:2, that his listeners are already familiar with the story that he has not yet told of Mary anointing Jesus' feet. It comes in 12:3–8. This is an indication that the author probably assumes much else and will not be telling these stories to his listeners for the first time. We know of Mary and Martha from Luke's famous story in which Jesus challenged Martha to see that women could also sit at the feet of Jesus and learn (Luke 10:38–42), probably highly relevant in congregational meetings, which will usually have been in someone's home where the woman of the house normally managed its affairs.

The author is probably responsible for some elements in the story that might be seen as problematic. These include that the reason given why Jesus did not respond straightaway was because he wanted to make an impact for God by resuscitating Lazarus, and so, let's Lazarus die first. It is an element essential to the drama. It recalls what he said in introducing the story of the healing of the blind man, that his blindness was set up so that Jesus could be shown to be the light of the world when he healed him (9:3). Another problematic element is the depiction of Jesus' praying out loud so people could hear and come to faith and telling God that was why he was doing so (11:42). These are the author's choices as he seeks to impress his listeners about Jesus, but some might say that in doing so he did Jesus a disservice, putting promotion and propaganda ahead of caring.

The drama is enhanced also by the detail that Lazarus had been dead for four days, reflecting the view held by many in the ancient world that in some sense death does not really reach completion until after three days. Many believed that the spirit hovered around the body until then. Well and truly dead and beginning to smell is an earthy element. There is a very human element also in the detail that Jesus was deeply moved and troubled, with the widely celebrated shortest verse in the Bible reporting, "Jesus wept" (11:35). For all the author's tendency to paint Jesus as larger than life through his stage-play technique, he does not embrace the view that the historical Jesus was not really a human being.

While the author is again at play in having the high priest unwittingly make a pronouncement about Jesus' death in 11:50, he may well reflect older tradition in reporting that the authorities had serious concerns about Jesus in the light of possible Roman responses. This is very plausible historically. The last thing the Romans wanted was instability on the vulnerable eastern flank of their empire. It had been breached by the Parthians in the previous century, which Herod, who later was installed as Rome's vassal king, helped to repel. Unrest had to be suppressed before it got out of hand and that might entail also putting restrictions on Jews practicing their faith, especially if it looked like it was part of the problem.

The Jewish historian Josephus mentions many movements—some military, some not, all with a religious background and some claiming their leaders were the Messiah—that the Romans needed to deal with. Passover weekend, when the city filled with pilgrims, was a particularly vulnerable time. Jesus fell into the category of the subversives, and Pilate crucified him beside two rebels, two other rebels as they would have seen it.

The danger for temple authorities, reflected behind the author's account, was that if the Romans saw them tolerating such disturbance, they might at the very least restrict their freedom and, worse still, destroy their temple, which they, in fact, did in 70 CE, in response to the great revolt. Informed Jewish leadership will therefore have certainly viewed popular movements such as that of Jesus and his followers with concern for fear of just how far the Romans might go with their sledgehammer tactics in suppressing dissent.

The author builds a picture in which the Jews, by which he means unbelieving Jews, are shown to belong to an absurd overreaction. Why would you want to kill someone who is healing people, even bringing them back from the dead! Why can't they see that Jesus had been sent as God's envoy, the climax of God's dealing with his people, and doing no more really than offering God's invitation to life! The dissenters don't come off well. They are hopelessly out of touch and are themselves therefore agents of the devil. We may not want to embrace the author's denigrations, but we can surely embrace the message of life and hope that he has Jesus bring, which can take us beyond the need to handle dissent and rejection in this way.

Reflection: What did it mean to claim that Jesus is the resurrection and the life, and what might it mean today?

Facing the End (John 12:1–50)

Listening to John

12:1 Six days before Passover Jesus entered Bethany, where Lazarus was living, whom Jesus raised from the dead. **2** They made a dinner for him there and Martha was serving. Lazarus was one of those reclining along with him. **3** So Mary took a pound of myrrh of nard, the real thing and expensive, and smeared it on Jesus' feet and wiped his feet with her hair. The house filled with the fragrance of the myrrh.

4 But Judas Iscariot, one of his disciples, the one going to betray him, commented, **5** "Why couldn't this myrrh have been sold for three hundred denarii and the money given to the poor?" **6** He said this not because he cared for the poor but because he was a thief, and as the one looking after their moneybag, he used to help himself to what people contributed to it."

7 So Jesus said, "Leave her alone. She got it so she'd have it for the day of my burial. **8** For you'll always have the poor with you, but you won't always have me."

9 A large crowd of Jews found out that he was there and came there not just because of Jesus but also to see Lazarus whom he had raised from the dead. **10** The chief priests had resolved that they would kill Lazarus, too, **11** because as a result of what happened to him many Jews had gone off and were starting to believe in Jesus. **12** The next day the big crowd which had come for the festival heard that Jesus was entering Jerusalem, **13** and so they fetched palm tree branches and went out to meet him and started calling out, "Hosanna! Blessed is the one who comes in the name of the Lord, the King of Israel!"

14 And Jesus found a young donkey and sat on it, as it is written, **15** "Fear not, daughter of Zion! Look, your king is coming sitting on the foal of a donkey." **16** His disciples didn't realize this at first, but, after Jesus was glorified, then they remembered that this was written about him and that they did this to him. **17** The crowd which was with him when he summoned Lazarus from the tomb and raised him from the dead had been testifying about him. [18] That's why the crowd went out to meet him, because they had heard that he had performed this miracle. [19] Therefore the Pharisees said to each other, "You see, there's no point; look, the world's gone after him."

[20] Now there were some Greeks who had gone up to worship at the festival. [21] They approached Philip from Bethsaida in Galilee, and were asking him, "Sir, we'd like to see Jesus."

[22] Philip went and spoke to Andrew. Then both Andrew and Philip went and spoke to Jesus.

[23] In response Jesus said, "The hour has come for the Son of Man to be glorified. [24] Truly, truly, I tell you, unless a grain of wheat falls into the ground and dies, it'll just lie on its own, but if it dies, it will produce much fruit. [25] Whoever loves his life will lose it, and whoever hates his life in this world will keep it for eternal life. [26] If anyone wants to serve me, let them follow me, and where I'll be, my servant will be, too. If anyone serves me, the Father will honor them.

[27] For now, I'm feeling troubled. And what can I say? Father, save me from this hour? But it's for this purpose that I've come to this hour. [28] Father, glorify your name!"

Then a voice came from heaven, "I have glorified it, and I will glorify it again."

[29] The crowd standing nearby, when they heard it, said "That was thunder." But others said, "An angel has spoken to him."

[30] In response, Jesus said, "This voice came not for my sake but for yours. [31] Now is judgment day for this world. Now the leader of this world will be deposed. [32] And as for me, if I am lifted up from the earth, I will attract all to come to me." [33] He was saying this as a way of indicating how he was going to die.

[34] The crowd with him responded, "We have heard from the Law that the Messiah remains forever. So how come you are saying that the Son of Man must be lifted up? Who is this Son of Man?"

[35] So Jesus told them, "The light will be with you for just a little longer. Walk around while you've got light, so darkness doesn't overtake you, because anyone walking in the dark doesn't know where they're going. [36] As long as you've got the light, believe in the light so that you may become children of the light." Jesus said this and then headed off to remain in seclusion from them.

[37] Despite his having done so many miracles in front of them they were not coming to believe in him, [38] so that the saying of Isaiah the prophet was coming true, who said, "Lord, who has believed what we have heard? And to whom has the Lord's arm been revealed?" [39] This is why they couldn't believe, because, again, Isaiah said, [40] "He has blinded their eyes, and hardened their hearts so that they mightn't see with their eyes and come to know with their mind and turn and he would heal them." [41] Isaiah said this, because he had seen his glory and was talking about him.

[42] Nevertheless, many of the leaders did come to believe in him, but they didn't admit it because of the Pharisees, so as not to be banned from the synagogue. [43] For they loved praise from people more than praise from God.

[44] Then Jesus made a proclamation and said, "Whoever believes in me, believes not in me but in the one who sent me. [45] And whoever sees me, sees the one who sent me. [46] I have come as light into the world, so that all who believe in me may not stay in the dark. [47] And if anyone hears my words and does not take them on board, I won't be the one judging them because I didn't come to judge the world, but to save the world. [48] Anyone rejecting me and not believing my words has something that'll be judging them: the word that I have spoken will judge them at the last day. [49] And I didn't come of my own accord, but the Father who sent me gave me instruction about what I should speak and say. [50] And I know that his instruction is about eternal life. What therefore I say to you, is in accord with what my Father told me, and that's how I tell it."

Thinking About John

The author's account moves now to Jesus' final days. It is where Mark begins his account of Jesus' last days. Mark has Jesus enter Jerusalem, look around the temple, then return to Bethany (11:1–11). He has him then go again the next day and perform his prophetic act in the temple, also symbolized by his cursing the fig tree for failing to bear fruit (11:12–25). Thereafter Jesus engages his critics (11:27—12:44), predicts the temple's downfall (13:1–37), and returns again to Bethany before making his final entry to celebrate Passover with his disciples. It was at that last stay in Bethany, according to Mark, that a woman anointed his head with oil (14:3–9). John knows that story and very likely was familiar with Mark's version of it but relocates it and gives it his own twist.

We have in fact four accounts of the woman anointing Jesus. Matthew's follows Mark's closely with just minor changes, such as identifying Jesus' disciples as the ones who complain, whereas Mark simply says it was those present with Jesus at the meal (Mark 14:3–9; Matt 26:6–13). John has Judas Iscariot do the complaining and suggests he was ripping the other disciples off. Luke has a version that portrays the woman as a sinner expressing gratitude to Jesus for having her sins forgiven and locates it earlier in Jesus' ministry (Luke 7:36–50). He also uses it to develop his picture of Jesus as engaging with sinners. The fact that all four stories have specific incidental links, as we shall see, makes it likely that they all go back to a single event that has been told and retold in various ways and for various purposes.

We may never really know what actually happened beyond that a woman approached Jesus with perfumed oil of myrrh, that there were complaints, and that Jesus did not agree. Mark has it take place in the house of Simon the leper. Luke's story also names the host as Simon, but portrays him as a Pharisee. Mark, Matthew, and John have it take place in Bethany, and all three include the complaint, that this was a waste and could have been sold for a lot of money, and the money be given to the poor, Mark and John mentioning three hundred denarii. They also agree in having Jesus respond, telling them to leave her alone and saying that they would always have the poor around to help but wouldn't always have him.

Mark and Matthew both say that what she had done was good, and Mark, that she had done what she could. Then both refer to the anointing as in effect anointing his body for burial, a motif that John brings in his own way, saying that she wanted to keep it for his burial, a little strange if she was now using it, but this is the author's playfulness. She anoints his body for his burial in advance. Mark and Matthew then mention that this story would be retold in her memory. Indeed, it was, and we are dealing with the outcome.

One of the major differences between Mark and Matthew, on the one hand, and Luke and John, on the other, is that the latter have the woman smear the oil on Jesus' feet and wipe them with her hair, whereas Mark and Matthew have the woman anoint Jesus' head. Anointing his head could be symbolic of Jesus' being anointed as the Messiah, the Anointed One. Was anointing of the feet originally what happened? The connection between anointing as messianic and anointing as a burial rite, reflecting normal procedures of anointing corpses before placing them in tombs, may have led to locating the story in Jesus' last days, rather than earlier as in Luke. We may never know.

Having a woman enter a meal scene and anoint someone would have been unusual, especially since all but John indicate that she was a stranger. While it is nowhere made explicit, there would be an issue of what a holy teacher was doing letting himself be treated in this way by such a woman. The use of oil might also make some think that this was something she used elsewhere in contexts of prostitution, making her action even more questionable. Only Luke suggests she is a sinner. He then removes the embarrassment of depicting Jesus as exposing himself to such an act of affection by telling us she was a sinner who had repented and was expressing gratitude. John's story also removes any embarrassment by depicting her as Jesus' friend, Mary. Mark does little to allay the likely embarrassment and so highlights the contrast between what the men would have felt and how Jesus treated her, namely, with dignity.

What might well originally have belonged to controversial stories about Jesus not distancing himself from questionable people, including women whom men feared and suspected, could still show through even in John's account where he has Jesus tell them to leave her alone. John's story, however, presents more of a domestic scene and connects to the previous chapter where Jesus has been with Mary and Martha and had raised Lazarus. John includes the story in Jesus' last days but gives it only limited attention, including to depict Judas as a crook. In Mark, it is simply those present who complain. In Matthew, it is the disciples. In Luke, it is a Pharisee. Mark's is probably closer to what happened.

John moves on from there to report the danger facing Jesus because of the impact the reports of his miracles were having, especially of his raising Lazarus, and the resultant growth in his popularity. The authorities wanted to clamp down on all and remove both Jesus and Lazarus.

His account of Jesus' final entry into Jerusalem follows Mark's in having Jesus riding on a donkey but differs from Mark in reporting that the disciples did not really appreciate what was going on until after Jesus' death and his return to God. He will have Jesus promise them that then they will understand things, and so they do, with the aid of the Spirit. John has him hailed as Messiah, King of Israel, by the crowd, but has the disciples not get it, somewhat difficult to imagine.

We see the author's playfulness with double meaning when he has the Pharisees declare that the world had gone after Jesus. For the author and his listeners, this would prove to be true in a deeper sense: through the gentile mission. They, themselves, were part of the evidence that this would indeed come true. This universal mission stays in view in what follows as the author immediately mentions some Greeks (a term used broadly for Greek-speaking foreigners) approaching Philip, assumed to be bilingual as an inhabitant of Bethsaida on the northwest side of Galilee, and wanting to see Jesus. This makes sense in terms of language, although the author in his revamping of the call of the disciples had reported that Peter and Andrew also hailed from Bethsaida (1:44), which he perhaps had forgotten, and is contrary to evidence elsewhere, which depicts Capernaum as their home (e.g., Mark 1:29–31).

It may at first seem unrelated that Jesus' response is to speak of the hour having come for the Son of Man to be glorified, until we recognize that these are the author's favored ways of talking about the event complex to be set in motion by Jesus' death. His death, seen literally as his being lifted up onto the cross, was for the eyes of faith the beginning of the process by which he would be raised and be lifted up to God, another typical example of the author's play with double meaning. He was to be glorified with God's presence, ascending where he was before he descended and became flesh. He would then have the Spirit sent which would not only enable the disciples to remember and understand what they had experienced in a new way but also inspire and empower them to go out into the world to win more disciples for Jesus.

That great event complex was about to begin and was the key to mission. The image of the seed needing to die, as their horticulture understood it, to be able to produce a harvest serves this end. Thus, Jesus' death will bring new life. The author then applies the same principle to the disciples, promising that if they do the same, offering their lives, they too will join him in his heavenly state.

After these important pointers to the future, the author brings a revised version of what he would have known from Mark as Jesus' distress in Gethsemane (Mark 14:32–42), an episode he omits. His adaptation has Jesus retreat from the vulnerability expressed in Mark and instead has him say something along the lines: Should I pray like that, as Mark has

Jesus pray? No. Because I came for this purpose (12:27). It fits the author's image of Jesus as in control, but at the same time, he is not reluctant to depict Jesus as being deeply disturbed. Earlier he mentioned that Jesus wept (11:35). Jesus would suffer. Jesus would be troubled, but the author always shows Jesus as confident and assured and will also want his listeners to be the same way. You suffer, but there need be no fear, because you have knowledge assuring you of future hope.

We then have another instance of the author's narrative play in reporting people's confusion about the voice from heaven and then depicting it as not something Jesus really needed to hear, but as a divine ploy for the purpose of promoting Jesus' special status, just as he did in the last chapter when he had Jesus pray, just so people could hear. For the author, Jesus needed no such assurance.

The author shifts back to the theme of Jesus' death and its significance in 12:31, hailing it as in some sense judgment day. In 16:8, he will return to this. In effect, the cross would expose sin and evil, on the one hand, as well as love, on the other, and so would expose this world's leader, the devil, potentially disempowering him. Jesus continues using his favorite language when speaking of his death, when he refers to his being lifted up, deliberately ambiguous with double meaning, referring to both his crucifixion and his exaltation as a result. With this, the theme of mission returns as his exaltation will lead then to the empowerment of the Spirit through which he will potentially attract or at least draw all to follow him (12:32).

The significance of the event is further underlined as the author has Jesus respond to the issue of why, as the Messiah, he was going to be crucified as Son of Man and how this all fitted together (12:34). He has in fact already been giving explanations, so, instead, has Jesus return to the imagery of light (12:35-36), which he had used to great effect in earlier chapters (9:5; 11:9-10).

Citing his many miracles (12:37), it sounds like the author is now advocating the miracle-based faith which he depicts usually as inadequate, but more likely, his meaning is that they should have used the miracles to perceive who Jesus truly was and so come to that kind of informed faith. Mark had used the vision of Isaiah in which God had declared in frustration that Isaiah was to face rejection and to rationalize it as God's intent (Isa 6:9-10). Mark used it in dealing with the experience of rejection after citing the parable of the sower (Mark 4:10-12). John uses it here also to complain about failure to believe (12:38-40). John asserts here that Isaiah had in fact seen Jesus, perhaps suggesting that it was in fact Jesus whom Isaiah saw in his vision.

The author may well have his current context in mind or its recent history when he writes of some senior people in leadership who had come to believe in Jesus but had not admitted it openly (12:42), adding that their fear was being banned from the synagogue (repeated similarly in 9:22 and 16:2), a tell-tale detail indicating that he was thinking of his own context not of the Jerusalem temple context.

The author brings this section to a close by having Jesus in a way summarize his own significance. He makes it very clear that he sees Jesus as not engaged in self-promotion, but in promotion of God, as any reliable envoy would be. It is an important and helpful perspective that reminds us that all the claims about himself as bread, light, and life, and much else, are in reality claims not about himself but about *God*. This is the golden thread which runs through the Gospel.

The author had spoken about Jesus' death as a moment of judgment, of exposure. Here he returns to the traditional notion of a day of judgment in the future. What will expose people will be their response to his message, which, again means ultimately their response to God. Jesus is God's agent, yes, God's Son, the embodiment of God's Word and Wisdom, but ultimately *God* is the focus.

This is one of a number of points where the author makes God the center. In doing so he has used images of universal appeal, reflecting key elements for human existence, water, bread, light. In doing so he has transformed the story of the Jewish Jesus, who in the other Gospels speaks the language of Jewish hope and faith, and made him the bearer of what is essentially the being and nature of God. It has made his Gospel of universal appeal and also helped open a path towards seeing God primarily in such universal terms, and as loving, and then also recognizing this understanding of God wherever it genuinely occurs across all cultures, beyond where the author could go.

Reflection: What is the golden thread that runs through John's Gospel and is visible again here?

4

Famous Last Words

Love—All the Way (John 13:1–38)

Listening to John

¹³:¹ Before the Passover Festival, Jesus, being aware that his hour had come to leave this world and return to the Father, having loved his own who were in the world, loved them to the end. ² And when the meal was in progress, after the devil had already planted it into the mind of Judas, son of Simon Iscariot, to betray him ³ and aware that the Father had put everything into his hands and that he had come from God and was going to God, ⁴ Jesus got up from the meal and took off his outer garment and taking a towel wrapped it around his waist. ⁵ He then poured water into a bowl and began to wash the feet of his disciples and to wipe them with the towel he'd tied around his waist.

⁶ So he came to Simon Peter, who said to him, "Lord, are you really going to wash my feet?"

⁷ Jesus answered, "What I'm doing you don't understand now, but after all this you will understand."

⁸ Peter said to him, "You're never going to be washing my feet."

Jesus replied, "Unless I wash you, there'll be no place for you with me."

⁹ Simon Peter said to him, "Lord, not just my feet, but also my hands and my head."

¹⁰ Jesus said to him, "Anyone who has had a bath doesn't need to wash except for their feet but is all clean; and you (disciples) are clean,

though not all of you." ¹¹ For he knew who was going to betray him. That's why he said, "Not all of you are clean."

¹² When he had washed their feet, putting on his outer garment again and sitting down, he said to them, "Do you realize what I have done to you? ¹³ You call me, teacher and Lord, and you're right; I am. ¹⁴ So if I your Lord and teacher have washed your feet, you also ought to wash one another's feet. ¹⁵ I have set you an example so that you might behave as I have behaved towards you. ¹⁶ Truly, truly, I tell you, a slave is not greater than his master nor is an envoy greater than the one who sent him. ¹⁷ If you realize this, you'll be blessed if you behave accordingly.

¹⁸ I'm not talking about all of you, because I know whom I have chosen, but this is so that the Scripture might be fulfilled which says, 'The one eating my bread has raised his heel against me.' ¹⁹ I'm telling you this now before it happens, so that when it happens you will believe that I'm the one. ²⁰ Truly, truly I tell you, whoever accepts anyone I shall send accepts me, and anyone accepting me accepts the one who sent me." ²¹ Having said this, Jesus was troubled in spirit and testified and said, "Truly, truly, I tell you, one of you will betray me."

²² The disciples looked at one another, not having a clue whom he was talking about. ²³ One of his disciples was reclining close to Jesus, the one he was fond of. ²⁴ So Simon Peter signaled to him to find out whom he was talking about. ²⁵ Leaning close to Jesus' chest as he was reclining there, he therefore said to him, "Lord, who is it?"

²⁶ Jesus replied, "It's the who I give the piece of bread to when I've dipped it." So dipping a piece of bread, he gave it to Judas son of Simon Iscariot. ²⁷ After he ate the piece of bread, then Satan entered him. Then Jesus said to him, "What you're about to do go and do it quickly!"

²⁸ None of those reclining there understood what he was really telling him to go and do. ²⁹ For some thought that because Judas handled the money, Jesus was telling him. "Buy what they needed for the festival," or for him to give aid to the poor. ³⁰ So having eaten the piece of bread, he immediately left. And it was night.

³¹ When, therefore he'd gone, Jesus said, "Now is the Son of Man glorified, and God is glorified in him. ³² [If God is glorified in him], God will also glorify him in himself, and glorify him immediately.

33 Little children I'll be with you for just a little while. You'll look for me and, as I told the Jews, 'Where I'm going you can't come,' I'm also telling you now. **34** I give you a new commandment, that you love one another; as I have loved you, that you also love one another. **35** By this everyone will recognize that you are my disciples if you have love for one another."

36 Simon Peter therefore, said, "Lord, where are you going?"

Jesus replied, "Where I am going you can't follow me now, but you'll follow me later."

37 So Peter said to him, "Lord, why can't I follow you now? I'll lay down my life for you!"

38 Jesus responded, "You'll really lay down your life for me? Truly, truly, I tell you, the rooster won't even have crowed before you'll have denied me three times."

Thinking About John

We have reached Jesus' final evening with his disciples. The author brings all he has said about Jesus so far into a simple and profound summary: "having loved his own who were in the world he loved them to the end." The famous John 3:16 begins with the statement: "God loved the world so much," and that is not to be forgotten when in the chapters that now follow the focus is on Jesus' love for his own. Love is the heart of the gospel, as the author captures it.

We are about to read five full chapters about what happened over Jesus' last evening spent with his disciples. Most of it is about what he told them. That is quite extraordinary but reflects the way the author wants to highlight the relevance of Jesus for people of his own time. It was standard practice in the ancient world when composing a biography of a famous person to give particular attention to what you envisaged that they would say to later generations as they came to the end of their lives. We even have whole documents devoted to imagining famous last advice, for instance, the *Testament of the Twelve Patriarchs*, completed probably by the end of the first century CE, which comprises twelve speeches by each of the twelve sons of Jacob.

Mark's final speech of Jesus addresses especially the destruction of the temple in 70 CE, an event close to his time of writing (Mark 13). Matthew reproduces it but with supplements that address problems in his context (Matt 24–25). Luke also reproduces Mark's material but leaves Jesus' final speech till he is with his disciples on their last evening together, as John, too, has done. For that purpose, Luke relocates some of the teaching found earlier in Mark (10:40–45) and turns it into Jesus' parting advice. It includes his teaching about himself as serving and how that sets an example for how the disciples should be (Luke 22:24–38). John 13 does the same in the author's own distinctive way.

The author is therefore drawing on tradition, which included such teaching but also included references to Peter's denial and Judas' betrayal. He frames his depiction of this last evening within his overall and constantly repeated image of Jesus as God's Son and envoy who came, sent by the Father, and is to return to the Father. The return is now the big event in focus, for it is about to happen. It is "the hour," as he often describes it, and now it has come and will play itself out in the sequence of events to follow. Judas' betrayal will trigger it, and so the author begins with reference to that act and to the overall framework, namely "that the Father had put everything into his hands and that he had come from God and was going to God" (13:3).

In the Greek, 13:2–4 is all one long sentence whose action does not begin until verse 4 where Jesus begins to wash his disciples' feet. Typically for the author, there are many possible levels of meaning. Literally, washing feet would normally happen as you arrived at someone's house, because you would get dirty feet walking on the dusty and dirty roads and paths. It was also customary that people going up to Jerusalem for Passover would take a purification bath in one of the immersion pools, as the author mentions in chapter 11, "Now the Passover of the Jews was near, and many went up from the country to Jerusalem before the Passover to purify themselves" (11:55). We may assume that Jesus and the disciples would also have undergone this ritual purification. In addition, washing could be a metaphor also for forgiveness of sins and not just ritual purification.

Allusions to any or all of this background may be in mind as the author tells this story. The striking aspect is not so much the washing, but that Jesus, himself, does it. Washing feet would normally be done by a slave or in a household without slaves, normally by the woman of the house. So in this sense the story is representing what Luke, too, made part of Jesus' final advice and where he has Jesus declare, "I am among you as one who serves" (Luke 22:27). This is Luke's rejigged version of what he found in Mark: "The Son of Man came not to be served but to serve and give his life a ransom for many" (Mark 10:45).

This focus on lowly service therefore goes back to the careful composition in Mark, which over three chapters has Jesus portray his way as the way of serving, suffering, and death. Mark contrasts this with the disciples' values who resist the notion, believing that if Jesus is Lord, then success, power, and victory was to be his lot, and theirs, and not brokenness and suffering. Thus, when in Mark, Jesus accepts Peter's acclamation that he is the Messiah, and goes on to speak of his embarking on a path of suffering and service, Peter counsels him that this cannot be, and finds himself rebuked by Jesus for being obsessed with typical human values instead of God's values (Mark 8:27–33).

In John's story we have, as it were, another version of Peter's error. Being Lord should not mean lowliness but the opposite. Jesus shouldn't be washing Peter's feet. So Peter gets it so wrong, but understandably so, given prevailing values of their time, which have survived well to our day. The author will go on to say that such lowliness and love is to characterize the disciples; otherwise, they can't be part of his community.

Peter gets it so wrong. He misses the point and wants a full wash, hands and head, too. The author will have us smile at Peter's naivete. The exchange helps clarify what is and is not meant to be symbolized in the washing of feet. One common interpretation is to see in it an allusion to the forgiveness of sins, which some see as John saying that this would be possible only after Jesus had died for our sins. The problem with that interpretation is that Jesus declares that they are already clean in that sense, all except Judas, of course, and later the author will have Jesus explicitly declare: "You are clean through the word I have spoken to you" (15:3). The reference to having bathed and therefore not needing to bathe again plays with the immersion ritual but uses it to symbolize their being clean in the more profound sense of forgiveness.

The upshot is that Jesus' action symbolizes not the forgiveness that they are allegedly yet to receive after his death, a misunderstanding, nor an act symbolizing his giving them forgiveness there and then, but an act of lowly love and affection. The author then takes precisely this up into what he goes on to say, namely their need to show the same attitude towards each other (13:12–17). Again, not an act symbolizing forgiveness, but an act expressing love. What Mark expressed so powerfully, namely that the Son of Man came not to be served but to serve and give his life a ransom for many (10:45), John has Jesus demonstrate in this act of love and affection. In that sense it also replicates the action of Mary towards Jesus.

It has always been hard to see greatness as love rather than power over others, especially since from time immemorial people have created images of God based on powerful men, whether as rulers of nations or as dominant fathers in families. Disciples in every age have so easily reverted to this model both of God and of themselves when assuming leadership.

This act of love does not take place in a vacuum. The author keeps reminding us of Judas and will also have more to say about the fallible Peter. There is also reference to a mysterious figure described as the disciple of whom Jesus was especially fond. Inevitably, some in attempting to overturn centuries of anti-gay prejudice have speculated whether we might have reference to a gay relationship here. In reality, it would have been very unlikely, given the prevailing values of the time, and seems rather to have more to do with a particular strategy of the author. One can embrace issues of justice for gays without trying to read it into the text when it is not really there.

We find the same figure referred to elsewhere, especially as being a source for the author's distinctive version of Jesus (21:20–25), in much the same way as later gospels appealed to special sources for their innovative portraits, such as Thomas or Philip or Mary Magdalene, all of whom have gospels composed in their name, and, allegedly, using them as their source. That is likely to explain the presence of this figure in John's Gospel, identified then later by a process of elimination and guesswork as, "must-be" John, so giving this Gospel its name.

The author's treatment of Judas also draws on the tradition we find in Mark and elaborated in Matthew and Luke, both in his Gospel and Acts. The author's version reflects his emphases, including that some people (his disciples) are chosen, and some are not (13:18), a way of explaining dissent and disbelief but, paradoxically, without implying they are destined not to believe and therefore are without blame. He also has Jesus appeal to Scripture (Psalm 41), another way of saying this was "meant to be" (13:18). It reads in full, "Even my bosom friend in whom I trusted, who ate of my bread, has lifted the heel against me" (Ps 41:9). He also depicts Jesus as having miraculous foreknowledge of what was to come and so tell his disciples that when it happens as he predicted then they should be convinced he really is the one (13:19).

The author then returns in 13:20 to have Jesus speak about positive responses to him and his message. It is a traditional saying that we find attested elsewhere (Matt 10:40). It reflects the widely accepted assumption that to accept people's authorized envoys amounted to accepting the senders, themselves. The saying has Jesus apply it to himself as sent by God, but also to those whom he will send, namely the disciples. The envoy model was fundamental to communication in the ancient world. Without the magic of telecommunication, that is how it had to be. Envoys had to act and speak for the ones who authorized and sent them on their behalf. It is the main model the author uses of Jesus, so that acceptance or rejection of Jesus as God's envoy equates to acceptance or rejection of God, a very God-centered model.

Such confident foreknowledge of what awaits him does not, as the author sees it, exempt Jesus from being troubled by it. So, he pictures Jesus as troubled, as he had in redeploying the Gethsemane tradition back in 12:27. This is also the Jesus who wept at Lazarus' death (11:35). Knowing what awaited him did not mean that Jesus was exempt from anguish about what he was about to face. For all the lofty claims the author makes about Jesus as the eternal pre-existent Son of God he never sees that as requiring that he deny that Jesus felt troubled. The author will also want his listeners to hear a similar message, at least to the extent that they could be confident about their ultimate reward.

John follows Mark in indicating that when Jesus predicts that a betrayal would happen, his disciples did not know who was to be the betrayer, but with one exception: the favored disciple. Judas takes the piece of bread and goes, and the rest have no idea why, nor see it as unusual. The incidental reference to giving to the poor is an indicator that the author assumes that care for the poor belonged to what Jesus and the disciples embraced as a value.

They were sharing a meal with bread, eaten piece by piece and apparently distributed by Jesus, taking the role of father/host, and dipping it in liquid of some sort, in wine mixed with water? Nothing suggests the actions that formed the ritual of Holy Communion are at play at this point, although the author knows the ritual, as is reflected in John 6:51b–58. Might the author intend that we do see such a reference, here, creating a parallel close to home for his listeners who might also know of members who shared that meal only to go and betray them to the authorities? We may never know. The author tells us Judas went out into the night, also a symbolic reference.

Having described Judas' departure, the event that would set off the process of events leading to Jesus' death, the author has Jesus return to familiar language, speaking of himself as the Son of Man and of his glorification (13:31). In a slightly awkward sentence, which someone later sought to clarify by an addition at the beginning of 13:32, preserved in later manuscripts and included in our translation in brackets, Jesus speaks of being glorified. Some have seen it as a paradoxical statement that defiantly describes the crucifixion as the moment of glory, a dramatic irony, but more likely it refers to the fact that the complex event now unfolding would lead Jesus back to the Father, exalted to glory, an event that would also bring glory to God because Jesus had stuck on the path of obedience to God's will.

This then returns us to the motif of the hour with which the author began in 13:1 and similarly he returns to refer to Jesus' going to the Father and to love. The new command to love in 13:34–35, modelled on Jesus' loving his own to the end (13:1), has been a key theme thus far and is the core meaning of Jesus' washing his disciples' feet. The author then has Jesus in 13:33 return to what he had said back in 7:34 to the Jews about going away and their not going to be able to find him. It evokes another response from fallible Peter, who is shown failing to understand that Jesus was talking about his death. John's listeners might well smile at his fallibility.

There is an important difference between what Jesus said to the Jews and repeats in 13:33 and what he then goes on to say to Peter. Peter will in fact follow Jesus, as will the disciples. This notion was expressed already in 12:26 ("If anyone wants to serve me, let them follow me, and where I'll be, my servant will be, too"), and it is in the climax of Jesus' prayer for his own in 17:24. Peter again misses the point, only to be told of his denial of Jesus three times, even before the rooster has crowed to indicate morning, using a detail found in his tradition. Like Matthew (26:34) and Luke (22:34), John corrects it from "before the rooster crows twice," as in Mark 14:30, to simply, "Before the rooster crows." In John 21 the author will mention Peter's martyrdom, depicted in legendary sources as his being crucified upside down. He will indeed follow Jesus in that sense too—another example of the author's serious playfulness.

John 13 is but the beginning of the extended portrayal of Jesus' last words. In it the author encapsulates core values represented by Jesus, love and love in leadership rather than self-serving leadership. He follows Mark's line of depicting Peter as well-meaning but lacking insight and does so in a way that is typical of his seriously entertaining dramas. In the following chapter he has other disciples, like Thomas, Philip, and the other Judas, ask more such questions, eliciting key insights about who Jesus is and also about the significance of the event now underway.

The fact that the author begins his five chapters of Jesus' final words to his disciples with the need for mutual love and ends them in John 17 with a prayer for unity and togetherness and keeps emphasizing it throughout these chapters very likely means that the author saw a need to do so. We might then wonder what kind of division or lack of love among disciples was going on in his setting that it needed so much attention?

Reflection: What might love have meant for the disciples and for the early listeners to John's Gospel and what might it mean for us today?

"Don't Let Yourselves Get Stressed and Anxious!" (John 14:1–31)

Listening to John

¹⁴:¹ Don't let yourselves get stressed and anxious! Trust in God and trust in me. ² There's lots of accommodation in my Father's house. If it were not the case, would I have told you that I'm going to get a place ready for you? ³ And if I'm going to get a place ready for you, I'll come again and get you to join me, so that you can be with me where I am. ⁴ And you know the way to where I'm going.

⁵ Thomas said to him, "Lord, we don't know where you're going; how can we know the way?"

⁶ Jesus replied, "I am the way and the truth and the life; no one can come to the Father except through me. ⁷ If you've got to know me, you will also know my Father. And now you do know him and have seen him."

⁸ Philip says to him, "Lord, show us the Father, and we'll be satisfied."

⁹ Jesus said to him, "Have I been with you all this time and you haven't recognized me, Philip? Anyone who has seen me has seen the Father. How can you say, 'Show us the Father?' ¹⁰ Don't you believe that I am in the Father and the Father is in me? The words I speak to you, I don't say of my own accord. It's the Father who abides in me doing his works. ¹¹ Believe me, that I am in the Father and the Father in me. Otherwise, believe because of the works themselves. ¹² Truly, truly, I tell you, anyone believing in me will do the works that I do, and they'll also do greater works than these because I go to the Father. ¹³ And whatever you ask for in my name I will do, so that the Father may be glorified in the Son. ¹⁴ If you ask anything in my name, I'll do it.

¹⁵ If you love me, follow my instructions, ¹⁶ and I will ask the Father and he will give you another helper, to be with you forever, ¹⁷ namely, the Spirit of truth, whom the world cannot accept, because it neither sees it nor recognizes it, but you recognize it, because it

remains with you and will be in you. [18] I'm not going to abandon you to be orphans; I'll come to you. [19] In a short while the world won't see me anymore, but you will see me; because I live, you will live, too. [20] On that day you will recognize that I am in my Father, and you are in me, and I am in you. [21] Those who have my instructions and keep them, they're the ones who love me, and those loving me will be loved by my Father, and I will love them and show myself to them.

[22] Judas (not Iscariot) asked him, "Lord, how come you're going to show yourselves to us and not to the world?"

[23] Jesus in response said to him, "Those who love me will keep my instructions, and my Father will love them and we will come to them and take up residence in them. [24] Those who don't love me don't hold to my words, and the message you are hearing is not mine but my Father's, who sent me. [25] I have spoken these things while remaining with you. [26] The helper, the Holy Spirit, whom the Father will send in my name, he will teach you everything and remind you of everything I have told you.

[27] Peace I leave with you, I'm giving you my peace; I'm not giving it to you the way the world gives it. Don't let yourself get stressed and anxious! [28] You heard that I said, 'I'm going away and coming again to you.' If you loved me, you'd be glad, because I'm going to the Father, because the Father is greater than me. [29] And now I have told you this before it happens, so that when it does, you may believe. [30] I'm not going to talk with you much anymore, because the ruler of this world is coming and he's got nothing on me, [31] but to let the world know that I love the Father and I'm following his instructions to me, get up, let's move on from here."

Thinking About John

The author is telling the story of Jesus and the disciples and so enters into what they are likely to have felt. This is a continuation of the conversation begun in chapter 13. Such feelings would also have been real in the author's own day. So Jesus' response to his disciples would be just as relevant for them. Don't get stressed and anxious; learn to trust. Ultimately, hope is based on trust, even in face of the unknown. One might argue that we need no more detail than that ultimately, we go into the hands of God and God cares. Can we know more?

In the conversation that Jesus is having with his disciples, the author highlights Jesus' role as being God's agent and envoy. He uses the image of a household offering permanent hospitality as a way of speaking of hope. He also has Jesus reassuring his disciples, not only that there is such hope but that he is going to ready the accommodation for them, playing with the metaphor, and then saying that he would then come and get them.

This image of Jesus may well have its origins in the early years of the Jesus movement when there was a strong expectation that history was about to come to its climax with divine intervention and the return of Jesus. Paul thought so, when he wrote of himself and the Thessalonians as: "we who are alive, who are left until the coming of the Lord" (1 Thess 4:15). Mark, too, envisaged that it would happen in his generation (Mark 9:1; 13:30). This is the first of only two places where John has Jesus give expression to this traditional view. The other place is in his final chapter, where he has Jesus refer to a belief that had arisen that, unlike Peter, the especially loved disciple might survive until Jesus' return, but John then corrects it. The fact is that Jesus did not return in their lifetime.

Had expectation of Jesus' return in their lifetime been the center of their faith, one can imagine that its failure to eventuate would have created a crisis of faith. It still hasn't happened two thousand years later! The reason why faith did not collapse was because its basis was not a future event but a person, namely God, and faith in God's goodness. In John 14 the being of God, referred to as the Father, is clearly also the basis for the author's faith. So, while he retains this traditional idea, he overlays it with meanings that shift the focus away from that event.

The reassurance that the disciples will join him—now, after their death—remains, as he just promised to Peter that he would follow him in that sense (13:36). While not abandoning the notion of a future coming of Jesus as part of the event called "the last day," the author now puts the focus on Jesus coming already to the disciples through the Spirit, as he will go on to explain in this chapter.

Already in John 13 the author employs the tactic of having various disciples ask key questions, often rather naively as Peter had done. Here, as that conversation continues in John 14, it is Thomas who asks the next question. He has not yet grasped that the language of going away was Jesus' way of speaking of his death. If you don't know where he's going to, you are of course not going to know anything about the way there! John's listeners would smile again as many times before.

The response to Thomas' question brings a major statement that makes an exclusive claim (14:6). In the process, by implication, Jesus makes it clear that he is going away through death back to the Father. The declaration states that only those who come to faith in Jesus will make it to the Father. The focus is the future, going to be with God after death, but it is equally applicable, as the author portrays it, to the present. Access to God is only through Jesus. This is an exclusive claim.

A less exclusive appropriation of at least some aspects of the declaration would be to say that the only way to come to God is to come to God the way Jesus portrays God, namely as offering a relationship of acceptance and love. Then one could argue that wherever we see and hear of God presented in the way Jesus presented God, and only there, even in contexts where Jesus himself might not feature or be named, we recognize the way to God. That is exclusive in the sense of claiming that only such a picture of God is true but allows us to be open to acknowledge that one culture or one religion does not have a monopoly on such an understanding of God. If we see it like this and as appropriate for our multicultural world, we should not, however, claim that this was the author's view. His view was exclusive. Rather, we can claim that the love also central to his message takes us wider than in his setting he would contemplate.

What follows this declaration expounds it not in terms of the future (as after death) but in terms of the present. For it has Jesus declare that to know and see him is to know and see God. The author again employs the strategy of having a disciple, Philip, ask a key question, again naively—for listeners to smile (14:8). Jesus' statements might appear to be claiming absolute identity: he is the Father; he is God! But that is clearly not the intent. Instead, the author portrays Jesus as God's envoy, not just like prophets or other human beings, but the Word/Wisdom of God embodied in the human person Jesus, whose words and deed are totally derived from the Father. The language of being "in" another person (14:11) is a way of speaking of intimate personal connection and will be used also of Jesus' relationship with the disciples, deep mutual connection and relationship.

At 14:12 the author shifts focus from who Jesus is to what his disciples would do. He had just spoken of Jesus' deeds and now makes the surprising claim that the disciples would do more, "greater" deeds. The reference is not to more fantastic miracles, but to more extensive outreach. It is about mission, including mission to the wider world. That is then the setting for the assurance of help as they pursue that mission. It is not a promise to answer all prayer requests ever, like people wanting big cars, lots of wealth, or other such ambitions. It is all about following the instructions, the commandments, of Jesus to make him known, and it is here that the author has Jesus promise someone to replace him, namely the Spirit.

An essential element in the author's story of Jesus is that through his death he would return to the Father and that God would then send the Spirit to help the disciples carry on. The word initially used of the Spirit in 14:16, *parakletos*, has a range of meaning, including helper, encourager, comforter, advocate. The author implies that these are equally applicable to Jesus, because he has Jesus speak of the Spirit as "another" helper (14:16). When Jesus then declares that the Spirit was with them and would be in them, it is likely he refers to the fact that through Jesus, as bearer of the Spirit, the Spirit was "with" them but would one day be "in" them (the "in" language again).

Already at this point the author indicates that on that day, from that day on, they would know things that until that point they had not known. The author will spell that out in his next reference to the Spirit in 14:27 when he has Jesus tell the disciples that the Spirit would enable them to recall what Jesus taught, and, in that sense, also make it possible for the author to write his Gospel.

The author moves from the benefit of the coming of the Spirit to the subject of Jesus' coming again (14:18), but now gives it an interpretation that sees it occurring when the Spirit is given. The presence of the Spirit in the disciples could also be seen as the presence of the Spirit of Jesus and the presence of God (14:21). This is a very flexible use of language. People ever since have used a range of ways of speaking of God in their lives: the Spirit, Jesus, the Spirit of Christ, God, all in effect meaning the same.

The author expands upon this idea, his way of reworking the notion of Jesus' coming again, which he had introduced in 14:3, by having Judas (the other Judas, not the betrayer) ask how come Jesus would show himself to them and not to the world (14:22). Again, we may assume that the author would have expected his listeners to have grasped the point by now and so might smile again. In what follows the author has Jesus make it very clear: those who embrace the task of mission will know the presence of God and Jesus (14:23). Here the author uses the same word he had used in 14:2 about accommodation (*moné*) in his Father's house and swaps it now to refer also to God and Jesus finding accommodation (*moné*) in the life of the believer! To avoid any imbalance or any misunderstanding that Jesus is equating himself with God, the author then has Jesus restate his dependence and subordination in 14:24: he is God's envoy.

In 14:25 the author has Jesus return to the contrast between the present and the future. He is with them now, but the Spirit will be with them in the future and help them and teach them. Unlike in 14:16–17, where the author has Jesus speak of the Spirit as "it," he now has Jesus speak of the Spirit as "he." He is the helper sent to replace Jesus, but that role is defined. It is to put the focus on Jesus and who he was, not to be an independent operator. The author shows himself very aware that much that was said about Jesus arose in reflection on his life after his death and resurrection, when people saw him in a new light. It is crucial also for the author's own self-understanding and the status of his work, that he claims that what he was saying about Jesus was inspired by the Spirit, including the creative way he painted Jesus' portrait.

John 14 ends as it began, with the same instruction, "Don't let yourself get stressed and anxious!" (14:1, 27), but instead, embrace peace. The foundation for such peace is the knowledge that he challenges them to grasp, namely that he is going to God and God is greater than he is and is the basis of all hope. He slips in the reference to predictions coming true, as he has done before (13:19), and then rounds off the conversation by pointing to the fact that the world ruler, meaning its spiritual ruler, the devil, was circling and they should stop and move on.

It looks very much like this might have indeed been the end of Jesus' parting words to his disciples at some stage in the development of the Gospel. They are to get up and go. We might then go straight from the end of John 14 to the beginning of John 18 where they accordingly get up and go and make their way to the Mount of Olives. If that was how the Gospel once read in an earlier version, now the author has expanded Jesus' farewell advice by adding three more chapters. In them he returns to his theme of unity and love, clearly a major concern that, it seems, he must have felt needed more attention.

John 14 has often been used in funeral services, especially its opening verse, best known in its traditional translation, "Let not your hearts be troubled" and "In my Father's house are many mansions." While the author's saying is shaped by the tradition of promising Jesus' second coming to gather his own, it is usually heard as promising hope for life after death.

This is not inappropriate because the author does write at many levels, and one is certainly the belief that the disciples would also follow Jesus on his journey through death to life with God.

Older Jewish tradition, reflected also among the first generations of followers of Jesus, saw life after death as a state of sleep or semi-consciousness, awaiting the day of resurrection. This is Paul's understanding, for instance, who expects to be still around when that day came. As time went on, however, there developed the sense that those who had died were not in a sleeping limbo but were with God and with Jesus and with some consciousness. We see this in Luke, who has Jesus tell his co-crucified victim that that very day they would meet again in paradise (Luke 23:43) and has Jesus tell the parable of the rich man and Lazarus which assumes even that judgment effectively sorts people at death (Luke 16:19–31).

John's Gospel also assumes that life after death is with full consciousness, even though it can still have Jesus speak of a judgment day and of future resurrection on that day (5:28–29; 6:39–40). When he has Jesus declare that he is the way to the Father, at one level this refers to following him on the way to God after death. Typically for our author, however, it can also mean coming into a relationship with the Father in the present, before death, as he goes on to argue. It may seem a little messy to have multiple meanings like this, until we realize that really the focus is not time and place, that is, a last day or a location after death, but a *person*, namely the person of God. For hope has God as its focus, the God who loves, so whatever the time and place, people can rest their faith on that foundation. This is the golden thread running through the Gospel, as we have seen.

What the author has Jesus offer within the story as comfort and challenge to his disciples, the author would have seen as at the same time a message of comfort and encouragement to followers of Jesus in his own day. It pointed them to hope in God, as portrayed by Jesus, and to engagement in the task of continuing Jesus' mission in partnership with the Spirit, and did so in a way that has continued to speak to generations of Jesus' followers down through the centuries.

Reflection: What really is the basis for hope and confidence according to this chapter?

Love and Hate (John 15:1–27)

Listening to John

15:1 I am the true vine, and my Father runs the vineyard. **2** Every branch in me that does not bear fruit he removes. And every one producing fruit he cleans up so it will bear more fruit. **3** You are already clean because of the message I have given you. **4** Stay connected to me, and I to you. As a branch cannot bear fruit of its own accord except it stays connected to the vine, so you can't, unless you stay connected to me. **5** I am the vine, and you are the branches. Everyone staying connected to me and me to them bears fruit because, unconnected to me, you can't produce anything. **6** If someone doesn't stay connected to me, they're discarded like a branch and dry up and they get gathered up and thrown into the fire and burned. **7** If you stay connected to me and my words keep connected to you, ask whatever you want, and it will be done for you. **8** In this is my Father glorified that you bear lots of fruit and be my disciples.

9 As my Father has loved me, so I have loved you. Stay connected to my love. **10** If you keep my instructions, you will stay connected to my love as I have kept my Father's instructions and stay connected to his love. **11** I have said these things to you so that my joy may be in you, and you can be filled with joy. **12** This is my instruction to you, that you love one another as I have loved you. **13** No one has greater love than this, that they lay down their life for their friends. **14** You are my friends if you do as I have instructed you. **15** I no longer call you servants, because a servant doesn't know what his master is doing, but I have called you friends, because everything I heard from my Father I have made known to you. **16** You didn't choose me; I chose you and appointed you to go and bear fruit and that your fruit remain, so that whatever you ask the Father in my name he will do it for you. **17** This is my instruction to you, that you love one another.

18 If the world hates you, know that it hated me before it hated you. **19** If you were of this world, the world would love its own; but because you are not of this world and I have chosen you out of the world, that's why the world hates you. [20] Remember the word I spoke to you about a servant not being greater than its master. If they persecuted me, they will also persecute you. If they took my word on board, they'll also take yours. [21] They'll do all these things to you because of my name, because they do not recognize the one who sent me. [22] If I had not come and spoken to them, they would have no guilt, but now they have no excuse for their guilt. [23] Anyone hating me is also hating my Father. [24] If I had not done the works among them that no one else did, they would not be guilty. But now they have seen and have hated both me and my Father. [25] But this is so that the saying written in their Law may be fulfilled, 'They hated me for no reason.'

[26] When the helper comes, whom I will send you from the Father, the Spirit of truth, who comes out of the Father, he will testify on my behalf; [27] and you, too, will testify, because you have been with me from the beginning.

Thinking About John

We had seemingly come to the end of Jesus' final words to his disciples in 14:31, but here we begin again. The author uses the image of the grapevine. Prophets had used the image of a vineyard when confronting the people of their day (Isa 5:1–2) and Jesus, according to Mark, used it to confront the people of his day (Mark 12:1–12).

Wine was an important element of life then, and for wine you needed a good harvest of healthy grapes. The author has Jesus use it of himself and the disciples. He depicts Jesus as the vine and the disciples as the branches. It was all about staying connected. Maintaining grapevines in such a way that they bore fruit from year to year was a familiar image. You needed to remove awkward or broken branches and canes and clean the good ones up with some pruning to ensure they didn't get too straggly and would bear healthy bunches of grapes the following year.

In using this image, the author is tapping into the wisdom that behavior can be a fruit, an outcome of inner attitude and orientation. Matthew preserves such wisdom in having Jesus declare: a good tree produces good fruit; a sick tree does not (Matt 7:18). Paul wrote about love as a fruit of the

Spirit (Gal 5:22–23). This sense of deeds flowing not from efforts to keep commands but flowing from attitudes within has been a significant observation about how people can change. The emphasis is: stay connected and you will produce a good harvest of grapes; you will produce the right behavior—above all, love, which is also the basis for reaching out in mission.

The author does not specify what he means by fruit. Fruit bearing can mean winning others to become disciples of Jesus. In 12:19–24 the author has Jesus use it in the context of reaching out, including to the Greek-speaking world. This is probably in mind where he speaks here of bearing much fruit and links it to the promise of having prayers for help answered, as he had in the context of doing these greater works in John 14.

When the author writes of removing the unfruitful canes, which would then be gathered up and burned (15:6), was he hinting at the fires of hell? Possibly, but it is not usually an emphasis of his message. Typical of his style, the author uses the word "clean" both literally of cleaning up the various fruit-bearing branches of the vine, but also symbolically of being cleansed from sin. The focus is on bearing fruit and that this honors God because it is God's will that people have life. Grapes, grapevines, and vineyards belong to the world of celebration, so it is not surprising that the author has Jesus speak of joy and gladness (15:11).

The author emphasizes that staying connected implies taking on board the message of Jesus and in particular the instruction to love one another, which he makes explicit in 15:12 and 15:17. In between these verses he has Jesus illustrate what he says in 15:12, that they are to love one another as he has loved them. That love includes no longer calling the disciples servants but calling them friends and indicating the extent of that love for them by being willing to die on their behalf, an allusion to what awaited him, but also possibly an allusion to one of the aspects of its meaning, as a sacrifice for sins, also an element among the author's ways of interpreting Jesus' death.

He also has Jesus say that he had chosen them and commissioned them to bear fruit that would last, an allusion to mission. The language of being chosen has always been a way of affirming the joy of being loved, even though when removed from that rhetorical context it can become problematic, especially when employed as a device to explain why others reject you by saying that they were destined to be written off because they were not chosen—hardly, then, their fault when taken literally.

From 15:18 the author has Jesus turn to the prospect that the disciples were likely to face rejection, indeed hatred, prefigured in what was to happen to Jesus himself. This is stark and serious and must have had relevance also for the author's listeners. It not only warns them that they would face hate and even persecution. It also explains it by asserting that this will be because people of the world simply won't grasp what they are on about. It goes, however a little further, with particular reference to Jesus' own people. Echoing the words of the Gospel's beginning, "he came to his own and they did not accept him," he declares them guilty without excuse and cites, as the author puts it, their Law's own prediction as coming true; "They hated me without any reason," a formulation found both in Psalm 35:19 and in Psalm 69:5. The author here treats the Book of Psalms as belonging under the general heading of the Law, as he does also in 10:34. The next chapter will continue this focus on rejection and hate, where it goes on to comment about conflict with synagogue Jews.

This chapter concludes with another reference to the Spirit as the helper, but this time indicating that it was Jesus himself who would send it. The word used can also mean advocate as well as helper and this may well be the shade of meaning here, especially after the author has had Jesus speak of guilt. It would then also fit the description of its activity and the activity of the disciples as testifying. Testifying or bearing witness was also the language of mission and, as in John 14, links the sending of the Spirit to the sending out of the disciples in mission and outreach.

By the end of the chapter the imagery of the vine seems a long way back, but the assumption is that it is the Spirit that will enable the disciples to produce a rich harvest, an image of mission. To do so they will need to stay connected with the vine from which they will gain their nourishment and also hold together. The author assumes that being a follower of Jesus is not about having at some time past had a conversion and being assured of a place in heaven. It is about an ongoing relationship along with others in which one shares in the creative and healing love of God, both for oneself and for the world. We might use the imagery of marriage. A wedding counts for little if there is not an ongoing relationship.

Reflection: What understanding of being a follower of Jesus do you see in this chapter?

Hope and New Beginnings (John 16:1–33)

Listening to John

16:1 I've told you this, so you won't be thrown off course. **2** They will ban you from their synagogues, but, worse still, the time will come when anyone killing you will think they are offering a service to God. **3** They'll do these things to you because they have not come to know the Father nor me. **4** But I'm telling you all this now, so that when their time comes you will remember that I told you.

I didn't tell you about this to start with, because I was with you. **5** But now I'm returning to the one who sent me and none of you is asking me 'Where are you going?' **6** But because I have told you these things, grief has filled your heart. **7** But I'm telling you the truth, it's fitting for you that I go away. For if I don't go away, the helper won't come to you, but if I go, I will send him to you. **8** And when he comes, he will convince the world about sin, about goodness, and about judgment. **9** About sin because they don't believe in me; **10** about vindication because I'm going to my Father and you'll no longer see me; **11** and about judgment because the ruler of this world will stand condemned.

12 I've still got plenty to tell you, but you can't take it now. **13** When he, the Spirit of truth, comes, he will lead you into all truth, because he won't be speaking on his own behalf, but what he will hear he will tell you, and he will announce to you what's going to happen. **14** He will glorify me, because he will take what comes from me and tell you about it. **15** Everything which the Father has is mine. That's why I said that he'll take what comes from me and tell you about it. **16** In a little while you won't see me anymore, and again, in another little while you will see me."

17 Some of his disciples said to one another, "What's this he's telling us? 'In a little while you won't see me anymore and again in another little while you will see me'? and 'I'm going to the Father'?" **18** So they were saying, "What's this he's saying, 'A little while'? We don't understand what he's talking about."

¹⁹ Jesus realized that they were wanting to ask him, so he said to them, "Are you looking for an answer among yourselves about my saying, 'In a little while you won't see me anymore, and again in another little while you will see me'? ²⁰ Truly, truly, I tell you, you will weep and mourn, but the world will rejoice. You will be immersed in sadness, but your sadness will be changed into gladness. ²¹ When a woman is giving birth, she experiences pain, because her time has come, but when she gives birth to a child, she doesn't remember the trial anymore for the joy that a human being has been born into the world. ²² So you, too, will have sadness for the present, but I will show myself to you and your heart will rejoice, and no one will take your joy away from you.

²³ On that day you won't be asking me for anything. Truly, truly, I tell you, whatever you ask the Father for in my name he will grant you. ²⁴ Up till now you asked for nothing in my name. Ask and you'll receive that your joy may be complete. ²⁵ I have told you these things in the language of imagery. The hour is coming when I'll no longer talk to you using imagery but will tell you plainly about the Father. ²⁶ On that day you will ask in my name, and I'm not saying I'll ask the Father on your behalf. ²⁷ For the Father himself loves you because you have loved me and believed that I have come from God. ²⁸ I came from my Father and entered the world. Again, I am leaving the world and returning to my Father."

²⁹ His disciples said, "Look, now you're speaking plainly and you're not talking in images. ³⁰ Now we know that you know everything and have no need for anyone to question you. On this basis we believe that you came from God."

³¹ Jesus answered them, "Do you now believe? ³² Look, the hour is coming and has arrived when each of you will be scattered on your own and will abandon me, leaving me alone. But I'm not alone, because the Father is with me. ³³ I've told you these things, so that you may have peace. In this world you'll have hardship, but rejoice, because I have triumphed over the world."

Thinking About John

John 16 continues the theme of the opposition that Jesus tells his disciples they were to face. Being banned from synagogues reflects the fact that they were Jews, and probably also reflects what has happened at least in the history of John's listeners. The word synagogue refers primarily to a gathering rather than to a building. The projected opposition is fierce and potentially deadly and reflects a history of tension between the Jews who became followers of Jesus and his message and those who refused, a tension underlying the allegations in John 8.

The author then transitions to have Jesus speak about his going away. In doing so he plays with the notion of going away, its meaning being clear to his listeners, because it has already featured in his speech. The author, despite this, indicates that it was not yet clear to Jesus' disciples, and this builds drama and would evoke smiles. He then has Jesus identify their grief at what he has told them, including that he was going away (16:6), and explain that he has to go in order to have the helper, the Spirit, come (16:7).

The author has Jesus offer a neat summary of what the Spirit will do, namely convince the world about sin, vindication, and judgment. In effect, it is a reflection on the meaning of the event that lies before Jesus. His death is an exposure of sin. (Sin is to reject Jesus and so, God.) His exaltation is the sign that God affirms and vindicates him, in other words, declares he was right in what he claimed (or in traditional terms, that he was righteous). Then the condemnation in judgment on the world's power is in effect the result of its exposure in what happened to Jesus and therefore its disempowering.

This notion of judging and condemning the world's ruler, understood as the devil, is a creative reworking of what was a widespread view of what was to take place at the end of time, such as we see portrayed in the book of Revelation. Satan and his cronies are to be finally disempowered. Our author creatively depicts the cross as a moment of judgment because it exposes the devil for who he is and exposes sin for what it is.

The author then shifts further to address how the disciples would cope after he has gone and again the key is the sending of the Spirit. It almost sounds in 16:13 like the Spirit is now to add to what Jesus has been teaching and to take it a lot further, opening the door for new claims and new revelations about the future: "he will announce to you what's going to happen." It is possible to see also a promise that the Spirit might inspire visions of the future, but nothing the author provides suggests that this was his understanding. Instead, the Spirit will help them remember what Jesus said, as the author had already indicated (14:26), and help them also understand the full truth about who Jesus was (16:14). The author would doubtless say that his work illustrates the benefit. As with Jesus, the Spirit is not a loner, but is the envoy of God and also of Jesus, so it all comes back to presenting God. God's offer of life, presented in Jesus, is now re-presented by the Spirit in bearing witness to who Jesus was. This is the golden thread running through the Gospel.

In the section that follows there is a repetitive exchange over Jesus' saying that he would soon go but also soon be seen again. The author's listeners would know exactly what was meant, namely his death and resurrection, but the author builds dramatic effect by having the disciples not know and so, having his listeners smile yet again. It is imagery, and the author supplements the imagery by using a woman's painful contractions as an illustration. What on earth was Jesus talking about? The author's listeners know full well.

Before having Jesus explain, the author has him assure the disciples (and their successors) about prayer in the context of the mission on which they would be sent. It repeats what the author has had Jesus say earlier in 14:13–14 and in 15:16, so is clearly of importance for the author. The joy that they would experience in seeing Jesus raised from the dead is not the only joy promised them. There is also the joy of being heard in the context of mission. God, as the author sees it, wants people to be happy and find fulfillment, also a regular theme, emphasized earlier in 15:11 ("I have said these things to you so that my joy may be in you and you can be filled with joy").

Plain speaking comes, then, in 16:25, and again assures the disciples (and their successors) that God would heed their requests and respond to their needs after he leaves them. The author is pointing beyond his short absence until the resurrection. He is now talking about the ongoing absence of Jesus that would follow, when in one sense he would no longer be with his disciples and their successors, although in another sense he and God would be with and in them through the Spirit, as he had stated in 14:23.

The author then has the disciples affirm what was essential to understanding who Jesus was throughout the Gospel, namely that he came from God, as God's envoy (16:30). The author has Jesus end his advice to the disciples by indicating that they would flee and abandon him, but then assures them of peace, recalling his closing words in what may well have been an earlier version of his closing words, namely 14:27.

The claim in his final words, that he had triumphed over the world, amounts to repeating the essence of what had been said of the Spirit in 16:8–11, namely that it would convince the world of its sin, of Jesus' vindication, and the condemnation of this world's ruler, an exposition of the meaning of Jesus' death and resurrection. The cross would show the world's values up for what they really are, exposing sin as the rejection of love, a rejection the disciples, too, would share. They are assured that their choice to believe in him was the right one because it brought them into a relationship of peace with God.

Reflection: What is the basis of the assurance the author is having Jesus offer his disciples and so also to people listening to his Gospel?

Praying for Them and for Us (John 17:1–26)

Listening to John

17:1 Jesus spoke these words and then, lifting his eyes heavenwards, said, "Father, the hour has come. Glorify your Son, so that he can glorify you, **2** because you gave him authority over all flesh, to give eternal life to everyone you've given to him. **3** And this is eternal life, that they might know you, the one true God and Jesus Christ whom you sent. **4** And I have glorified you on earth, having completed the work you entrusted to me to do. **5** And now glorify me, Father, in your presence with the glory that I had with you before the world came into being.

6 I have made your name known to the people you gave me from out of the world. They were yours and you gave them to me, and they have kept your word. **7** Now they have come to know that everything that you have given me is from you, **8** because the words you gave me I have given to them, and they have accepted and come to know truly that I came from you and they have believed that you sent me.

9 I'm praying for them; I'm not praying for the world, but for those you have given me because they belong to you. **10** And everything that is mine is yours and yours is mine, and I have been glorified through them. **11** Now I'm no longer going to be in the world, but they are in the world, and I'm coming to you. Holy Father, protect them in your name which you have given to me, so that they may be one as we are one. **12** When I was with them, I protected them in your name, which you have given to me, and kept them safe, and none of them is lost except for the son of lostness, so that the Scripture might be fulfilled.

13 Now I'm coming to you and I'm saying these things in the world so that they might have my joy in full among themselves. **14** I have given them your word and the world has hated them, because they are not of the world as I am not of the world. **15** I am not praying that you remove them from the world, but that you protect them from the evil one. **16** They are not of the world as I am not of the world.

[17] Sanctify them by your truth; your word is truth. [18] As you sent me into the world, so I have sent them into the world, [19] and for their sake I sanctify myself so that they too may be sanctified in truth.

[20] I'm praying not just for them but also for all who will believe in me through their word, [21] that all may be one, as you, Father, are in me and I in you, that they, too, may be one, so that the world may believe that you sent me. [22] And the glory that you have given to me I have given to them, so that they may be one as we are one; [23] I in them and you in me, so that they may be fully one so that the world may know that you sent me and you loved them as you have loved me.

[24] Father, with regard to those you have given me, my wish is that they may be with me where I am, so that they might see my glory which you have given me because you have loved me from before the foundation of the world. [25] Righteous Father, the world has not acknowledged you, but I have acknowledged you, and they have acknowledged that you sent me; [26] and I have made known your name to them and will make it known, so that the love with which you have loved me might be in them and I in them.

Thinking About John

This wonderfully rich prayer, which the author has placed on the lips of Jesus, has been an inspiration down through the centuries, not least because it crystallizes much of what the author has sought to convey about Jesus and his significance in the preceding chapters. Like the farewell discourse that precedes it, the author has composed it to bring to expression what he believes would be Jesus' concerns for believers in his day and beyond.

People who have read the prayer through the lens of the Letter to the Hebrews with its image of Jesus as the great high priest, have called it Jesus' high priestly prayer, although nothing in what the author offers us suggests he saw it in those terms. At one point there is a reference to Jesus sanctifying himself, but that sits alongside a reference to the disciples also being sanctified, sanctified by truth (17:17–19). Sanctification is clearly an image for setting oneself aside to be able to perform an action on God's behalf, certainly applicable to priests but also to others.

The prayer is in part repetitive, not unlike the somewhat repetitive style of the previous chapter, but this also helps underline its key themes. Six times the author has Jesus refer to himself as sent by God and used it as a short summary of what people are to believe: "that the world may believe that you sent me" (17:21; similarly, 17:3, 8, 18, 23, 25). He is the sent one, who has come from the Father. Another constant is the reference to what the Son was sent to do, the work, the word, he was to perform and share. The word or message was the offer of eternal life and, as the open sentences make clear, that is not about a place or a reward, but about a person: knowing, being in relationship with God: "this is eternal life, that they might know you, the one true God and Jesus Christ whom you sent" (17:3). That has been the constant theme of the Gospel.

We find, too, repeated references to the status of those who have believed and so accepted that invitation, as those "given" to the Son by the Father and therefore kept from failing, echoing the promise in 10:28–29, that as sheep they would be kept secure. This language of being given and kept, like the language of being special and chosen, was, as we have seen previously, a way of expressing being loved. It always had the potential that it could be applied negatively to those who have not believed, declaring them not given, not chosen. Strictly speaking, if destined by God to reject, they should therefore carry no blame, but as we have seen, that is to misunderstand the function of such rhetoric. At most, however, we have a reference to Judas in 17:12, again as not kept, but by implication destined to betray, as foretold by Scripture, yet still assumed to be blameworthy.

"The world" also features regularly, meaning those who refuse to accept the offer of life and so embrace a set of values and norms that are in conflict with what Jesus presents. The author's concerns—not with history but with faith communities in his own day—show not only in the way he has Jesus pray for his disciples but above all in the way he has Jesus deliberately pray for future disciples.

The concern is not just that they remain believers and stay connected, but also that they uphold a sense of oneness and unity, another repeated theme (17:11, 21–23). That unity has its model in the relation between the Father and the Son, expressed as love and expressed through the language of being "in" the other, an expression of intimacy. Maintaining unity obviously mattered and was also seen as important for the wider world, which would thereby recognize love and might come to faith (17:21, 23). This call to unity echoes the new commandment to love one another with which Jesus' farewelling words began (13:34-35).

The distinctive and close relationship between Father and Son is regularly in focus. What is yours is mine and vice versa is one way of expressing it (17:10), but always with the sense that the Son obeys the Father not that the Father obeys the Son. Hence the language of authorization, being given the gift of believers, and being sent as the Father's envoy. Ultimately, as the opening sentences emphasize, it is God who is the source of life, not the Son, independently or as a second god, a misunderstanding that later creeds ensured would be declared invalid.

Another motif that comes through frequently is "glory." It was a way of speaking of the wonder of God's being that can also embrace others. The author's pattern for describing the Son's significance has him with God, sharing God's glory from before creation, referred to twice in this prayer (17:5, 24). It also has him return to this glory, his glorification, set in dramatic contrast to the humiliation of the cross. The prayer begins with the request to be glorified, to return to the Father, and the events now set in motion would indeed bring that wish to fulfillment.

"Glory" is a word with wide meaning which includes praise and so we find it used here also in that sense, that the Son and his future disciples would bring praise to God. Ultimately, the disciples, too, are to be with the Son in glory, a repeated theme in Jesus' farewell words (13:36; 14:3; also 12:26). They will ultimately follow him all the way, and this, here, is Jesus' prayer (17:24).

"Name" is also a word meaning more than a label. Its broader sense survives when we speak of someone acting in another's name, meaning their authority. That sense is present here as well as the notion of the name conveying who the person really is, so that the author has Jesus speak of giving his name or God's name to his disciples, in that sense, offering them a relationship if they believe in him, in his name.

Generosity and love show through in the request that the disciples and their successors find fulfilled joy (17:13) and ultimately find fellowship with Jesus in the presence of divine glory (17:24). Their path is to follow Jesus' path. That not only affects their end but also the interim of their life in the world. For they too are sent into the world with the same offer of life presented in Jesus. The author has Jesus speak of them as having already been sent, which fitted well the author's thinking of his listeners (17:18), even if within the narrative that was still to happen when Jesus met with the disciples on Easter Day (20:21).

This prayer brings it all together and espouses a view of faith community as characterized not just by belief and hope but also by love and unity. One might wonder if the special focus on unity may have been directed at a simmering disunity, which would manifest itself in the division about Jesus reported in 1 John 2:19.

Reflection: What do you see as the main concern that the author is having Jesus express, and what relevance might it have had then for the author's community and might it have for us today?

5

The End and the Beginning

Betrayal, Arrest, and Denial (John 18:1–27)

Listening to John

¹⁸:¹ Having said this, Jesus went off with his disciples to the other side of the creek that runs down the Kidron Valley where there was a garden, into which he and his disciples entered. ² Judas, who was to betray him, also knew the place because Jesus often got together there with his disciples. ³ So Judas, taking with him a band of soldiers along with officers from the chief priests and Pharisees, came there with lanterns and torches and weapons. ⁴ Jesus, therefore, knowing all that was to happen to him, went out and said to them, "Who're you looking for?"

⁵ They replied to him, "Jesus of Nazareth."

So he told them, "That's me."

Now Judas, the one going to betray him, was standing along with them. ⁶ When he told them, "That's me," they pulled back and fell to the ground.

⁷ So he asked them again, "Who're you looking for?"

They said, "Jesus of Nazareth."

⁸ In response Jesus said to them, "I told you, that's me. If you're after me, let these others go," ⁹ which was so that the word might come true which he had said, "Of those you gave me none of them is lost."

¹⁰ Then Simon Peter, who had a sword, drew it, and struck the high priest's slave cutting off his right ear. His name was Malchus.

¹¹ But Jesus said to Peter, "Stick your sword back in its sheath; the cup the Father has given me to drink, am I not to go through with drinking it?"

¹² The band of soldiers and its captain and the officers of the Jews arrested Jesus and bound him. ¹³ They took him first to Annas. He was the father-in-law of Caiaphas, high priest that year. ¹⁴ It was Caiaphas who had advised the Jews that it was fitting to have one person die on behalf of the people.

¹⁵ Simon Peter was following Jesus along with one of the disciples, and that disciple was known to the high priest, and he went in with Jesus into the high priest's courtyard. ¹⁶ Now Peter was standing near the gate outside. So the other disciple known to the high priest went out and spoke to the gatekeeper and brought Peter inside. ¹⁷ Then the female slave who was the gatekeeper said to Peter, "Aren't you one of this fellow's disciples?" He said, "I'm not."

¹⁸ The slaves and officers had made a fire and were standing around it because it was cold and were warming themselves. And Peter, too, was standing there with them warming himself.

¹⁹ So the chief priest asked Jesus about his disciples and about his teaching.

²⁰ Jesus answered, "I've spoken openly to the world; I've always taught at synagogue and in the temple, where all the Jews gather, and I haven't been saying anything in secret. ²¹ Why are you asking me? Ask those who have listened to me what I told them. Look, they'll know what I've been saying."

²² After he said this, one of the officers standing nearby slapped Jesus, saying, "Is that how you're answering the high priest?"

²³ Jesus answered, "If I've said anything bad, give me the evidence of what's bad. And if I have spoken rightly, why are you hitting me?"

²⁴ So Annas sent him off bound to Caiaphas, the high priest.

²⁵ Simon Peter was standing around warming himself, so they said to him, "You're one of his disciples, aren't you?"

He denied it and said, "I'm not."

²⁶ Then one of the high priest's slaves, a relative of the one whose ear Peter severed, said, "Didn't I see you with him in the garden?"

²⁷ Again Peter denied it, and immediately the rooster crowed.

THE END AND THE BEGINNING

Thinking About John

We now move to the account of Jesus' arrest. The author will have been familiar with the stories told in Mark and perhaps had other sources. Mark has Jesus and his disciples relocate to Gethsemane, as does Matthew, following Mark. John has them relocate to a garden on the other side of the Kidron Valley, thus to the slopes of the Mount of Olives, specifically mentioned as such in Luke. Traditionally we combine all this together and speak of the garden of Gethsemane.

In the other Gospels we then read of Jesus praying in anguish, seeking initially to be rescued from his plight: "Abba, Father, all things are possible for you. Take away this cup from me; but what matters is not what I want but what you want" (Mark 14:36). John has omitted this altogether and instead had brought a reworked version of it in chapter 12, where he presents a more confident Jesus who declares he would make no such request: "For now, I'm feeling troubled. And what can I say? Father, save me from this hour? But it's for this purpose that I've come to this hour" (12:27).

Instead, John's account moves straight to the arrest scene. Only he mentions the presence of soldiers accompanying the temple officers. This would suggest that already at this stage Roman authorities were involved. This would fit what many see as likely to have been the prime initiative leading to Jesus' execution, namely, the Roman administration's concern to quell all potential causes of unrest.

The initial encounter between Jesus and those coming to arrest him raises a few questions. They were shocked that there he was confronting them and so fell back. Is that what the author is saying or is their falling back something more? It is possible to translate Jesus' response, when they tell him who they are looking for, with the words, "I am he." Some then see this as a play on the name of God as Moses heard it at the burning bush, "I am, who I am" (Exod 3:14) and in Isaiah, which plays with the name of God as the great "I am" (Isa 43:10, 25; 48:12). Some, indeed, find an allusion to the great "I am" every time the author has Jesus say, as I have translated it, "It's me" or when he has him use it of imagery, such as "I am the light." Did therefore the use of the divine name cause their shock, according to the author? If that were so, one would expect some reference to it, and a similar reaction when Jesus repeats it here and uses it elsewhere, and then some reference to it, especially in contexts where his opponents cited his alleged blasphemies, but we do not. Therefore, it is more likely that what we have here is simply shock and surprise at his confronting them up front with "It's me."

When the author portrays Jesus as successfully persuading those arresting him to let the disciples go free (18:9), he cites Jesus' prediction or at least his prayer, that none of the disciples would perish, as finding fulfillment (17:12). This is part of reinforcing that Jesus is on side with God. The detail about one of their number lashing out at the high priest's slave and cutting off his ear was part of the tradition, but only here is the disciple named as Peter, and the slave named as Malchus, reflecting a tendency as time went on to give names to such figures, a tendency also seen in the identification of the woman who anointed Jesus as Mary. Only Luke, beside John, mentions that it was the right ear—memory or story elaboration?

To report such an action might raise problems in contexts where state officials could suspect danger, so it is little surprise that, except for Mark, the others have Jesus put a stop to it, from Luke's having Jesus say, "That's enough!" to Matthew and John telling the perpetrator to put his sword back in its sheath. Our author then uses what had been in the Gethsemane tradition, namely Jesus' speaking of his impending plight as a cup he must drink, and includes it in his telling Peter off (18:11).

The major difference between John and the other Gospels is the absence of a trial before the Sanhedrin. Having such a trial on Passover weekend was bad enough, but having it on the day of Passover and during its night hours, as Mark and so Matthew suggest (Mark 14:53–65; Matt 26:57–68), was so outrageous as to be unbelievable, so Luke at least transfers the trial to the morning, so during daylight hours (Luke 22:66–70). Was John's solution to delete it altogether? Did he instead have a kind of trial of Jesus at the hands of the Jews creatively spread throughout his narrative? Or did he know tradition according to which there was no trial but just a hearing before some of the key temple leaders? As often in historical reconstruction, we are left not knowing for sure.

Supporting the latter suggestion, that there was only a hearing not a trial, is the fact that the trial in Mark seems more like what Jewish Christ-believers would face in synagogues in his own time than what Jesus would have faced. The allegation of blasphemy for claiming to be the Messiah, and as such God's adopted Son, would not have been blasphemous, but would become so when by Mark's time that claim had taken on meanings that could well sound blasphemous, such as the accusations that Jews bring in John's Gospel.

In Mark there are two accusations, one related to the alleged claim to be Son of God, Messiah. The other is about the temple and Jesus' symbolic act confronting the temple and its authorities. Our author has the story about Jesus and the temple but puts it three years earlier (2:13–22). It looks very likely that he did this for thematic reasons, as we have seen, so that Mark's location of the event to Jesus' last days has a higher claim to reflect what actually happened. In Mark it is the foundation for the allegation that Jesus predicted the temple's demise. Mark then brings reference to this prediction three times, once in the trial before the Sanhedrin, once in the mockeries under the cross, and finally as symbolically fulfilled when the temple curtain rips at Jesus' death, a symbol of God's judgment. These elements, therefore, are missing in John's account.

In relation to the hearings, the author notes that Caiaphas was the one who suggested that it would be better to have one person killed than to have the Romans react with sledgehammer tactics, bringing chaos and destruction on everyone and potentially suppressing their religion (11:50). Part of the author's playful rhetoric was to have the high priest thereby unwittingly prophesy that Jesus would die for all in a different sense. If the literal sense reflects historical tradition, it would shed light on one possible motif for collusion between temple leadership and the Romans. Both would have had very different motives for having Jesus removed, the one, concerned about stability at all costs; the other, fearful of what that could mean if it got out of hand.

The Jewish hearing, as the author portrays it, does not raise the issue of blasphemy, such as the Jews in John were constantly raising, but simply asked about his teaching and leaves us with nothing of substance except what must be implied in what follows, where Pilate asks him about being King of the Jews. The Jewish authorities would have to have passed that allegation on to Pilate. Such is the logic of John's story.

It is highly likely that Pilate received such suspicions from sources available to him, and this would have put Jesus into the category of all such so-called Messiahs or would-be leaders promising change. Most would have been military, but not all, and from Rome's perspective, anyone who caused unrest and instability had to be gotten rid of. Unrest is unrest. One should not expect consideration of fine points of distinction.

On either side of the hearings before Annas and then Caiaphas in John's account is the tradition about Peter's denial, also part of the tradition. It would have rung bells with all who had subsequently saved their skin by denial of their faith or who had contemplated doing so. One element of the author's tweaking is to have a relative of the man who lost his ear to Peter be his final interrogator. The author's innovation is to match the three denials with the three questions Jesus asks the rehabilitated Peter in the final chapter, asking if he loved him and then authorizing him for leadership. The drama of failure becomes then the drama of grace and new beginnings.

Reflection: Why would the Roman administration want to get rid of Jesus, and what might that mean for people of John's day?

Jesus Before Pilate (John 18:28—19:16)

Listening to John

18:28 So they took Jesus from Caiaphas to the admin headquarters. It was early morning, and they didn't enter the headquarters so as not to be defiled but be able to eat the Passover.

²⁹ Therefore Pilate came outside to them and said, "What charge are you bringing against this fellow?"

³⁰ In reply they said to him, "If he weren't a criminal, we wouldn't have brought him to you."

³¹ Pilate said to them, "Take him away yourselves and judge him according to your law."

The Jews said to him, "We are not allowed to execute anyone." ³² This was so as to bring Jesus' prediction to fulfillment when he indicated by what death he was going to die.

³³ So Pilate entered the headquarters again and summoned Jesus and said to him, "Are you the King of the Jews?"

³⁴ Jesus replied, "Are you saying this of your own accord, or did others speak to you about me?"

³⁵ Pilate replied, "Am I a Jew? Your people and the chief priests handed you over to me. What have you done?"

³⁶ Jesus replied, "My kingdom is not of this world; if my kingdom were of this world, my supporters would fight to prevent my being handed over to the Jews. But now my kingdom is not from here."

³⁷ So Pilate said to him, "You are a king, then?"

Jesus replied, "You're saying I'm a king. I was born for this purpose and for this purpose came into the world, to testify to the truth. Everyone one who belongs to the truth listens to my voice."

³⁸ Pilate says to him, "What is truth?"

And having said that, he went out again to the Jews and said to them, "I don't find any grounds for convicting him. ³⁹ You've got a custom of having me free someone for you at Passover. Do you want me therefore to release for you the King of the Jews for you?"

⁴⁰ They shouted back again, "Not this fellow but Barabbas!" Now Barabbas was a rebel.

¹⁹:¹ So then Pilate took Jesus and had him beaten. ² And the soldiers plaited a crown from thorns and put it on his head and dressed him in a purple cloak ³ and kept coming up to him and saying, "Hail, King of the Jews," and they knocked him about.

⁴ And Pilate went out again and said to them, "Look, I'm bringing him out to you so that you can acknowledge that I find no reason to convict him."

⁵ And so Jesus came out wearing the crown of thorns and the purple cloak. And he said to them, "Look, here's the fellow!"

⁶ When the chief priests and the officers saw him, they shouted out saying, "Crucify him, crucify him!"

Pilate said to them, "You take him yourselves and crucify him. I find no fault in him."

⁷ The Jews therefore replied, "We have a law, and according to that law he ought to die, because he made himself out to be the Son of God."

⁸ When Pilate heard this said, he was all the more anxious. ⁹ And he went into the headquarters again and asked Jesus, "Where are you from?"

Jesus gave him no answer.

¹⁰ So Pilate said to him, "Are you not speaking to me? Don't you know that I've got the power to free you and the power to crucify you?"

¹¹ Jesus responded, "You wouldn't have any power over me unless it was granted you from above. Therefore, the one handing me over to you bears the greater guilt."

¹² From this point on Pilate sought to free him, but the Jews shouted, "If you free this man, you're no friend of the emperor. Everyone claiming to be a king does so in opposition to the emperor."

¹³ When Pilate heard these comments, he took Jesus outside and sat on the seat for announcing verdicts, at the place called the Stone Pavement, and in Hebrew, Gabbatha. ¹⁴ It was the day of preparation for the Passover, about midday. And he said to the Jews, "Look, here's your king!"

¹⁵ They then shouted, "Take him away, take him away! Crucify him!"

Pilate said to them, "Am I to crucify your king?"
The chief priests replied, "We have no king but the emperor."
¹⁶ Then he handed him over to them to be crucified.

Thinking About John

Mark has a simple exchange in which Pilate asks Jesus if he is the King of the Jews, to which Jesus replied, "You're saying so," and after that remains silent (15:1-5). Then Mark brings Pilate's offer to release him, but the chief priests call for Barabbas instead (15:6-15). After Pilate condemns him to death, the soldiers beat Jesus up (15:16-20). Beating up people declared guilty was a common pattern of abuse.

The author's creative skill is apparent in the way he has shaped the trial before Pilate. He creates seven scenes which alternate between having Pilate outside the praetorium, the administrative headquarters, talking with Jesus' accusers and having Pilate inside it talking to Jesus. He achieves this in part by explaining that the Jews would have otherwise defiled themselves and rendered themselves unable to participate in the Passover celebration the following night. The author has Jesus die on the so-called Day of Preparation before Passover Day which was to commence that Friday evening at sundown and run through to sundown on Saturday, the Sabbath, hence his calling it a special Sabbath.

This differs from the other Gospels which have Passover Day start at sundown on Thursday and run through to sundown on Friday, according to which, then, Jesus' last meal with his disciples took place in the context of the Passover meal on Thursday night and Jesus died on Passover Day. Did associating Jesus' last meal, the Eucharist, with the Passover meal lead to their dating or did seeing Jesus as slain when Passover lambs would have been slain determine John's dating? We do not know.

Whatever the history, the author's distinctive dating enables him to develop his drama in seven scenes of Pilate moving in and out of the praetorium. The first scene (18:28-31) is where Pilate asks why the temple authorities have brought Jesus to him, and in the fairly gruff exchange, they declare Jesus a criminal, and when Pilate tells them to exercise justice using their own legal system, they declare he's guilty of a capital offence—without in John's story saying why. This enables the author yet again to show one of Jesus' predictions coming true (12:33), namely about the nature of his death as at the hands of the Romans, so crucifixion, the Romans' method of execution, underlining for the listeners his super foreknowledge.

Scene two (18:33-38) has Pilate go inside and ask Jesus directly if he's the King of the Jews. This comes as no surprise when we know the story, but nothing thus far in John's story has mentioned that as the accusation. There is little doubt historically that Jesus was placed in the broad category of being a subversive. He was accused of being another would-be King of the Jews, equivalent of the Messiah, the Christ. That then eventually gave the movement its name, Christian. They would, of course, always have to explain that he wasn't what people normally meant by a Messiah, namely a military subversive or rebel.

While Mark's simple, "Are you the King of the Jews?" was followed by Jesus' brief answer, "You're saying so" and then his silence, the author of John removes the silence, replacing it by an exchange about kingship (18:33-38). It includes the intimation that it was the chief priests who passed that accusation on to him. This is part of the author's consistent attempt to lay the blame on the Jews, whereas already the presence of soldiers at Jesus' arrest, plus much more, indicates that the Roman administration had always been a major player and probably *the* major player in snuffing Jesus out.

The same agenda is reflected in the conversation that replaces Jesus' silence with the declaration that his kingship was not of this world, so, by implication, no threat to Rome's rule. Some have read it as implying that his kingdom was to be exercised only in heaven, but that is clearly not the author's view. It is about being born again and so entering the kingdom of God, as Jesus had told Nicodemus, and living in the community of faith and love in the here and now. That should be no problem for Pilate, at least not directly. To Pilate, but also to those hearing the Gospel, it was important to explain that it was not a subversive military movement.

The declaration that it was about truth sounded playfully philosophical and might have been heard as such by John's listeners, but this was just yet another way of saying what Jesus had been saying, as a golden thread running throughout this Gospel, namely that he came to testify about God and, on God's behalf, make the offer of life, in that sense, by being, as he told his disciples, the way, the truth and the life (14:6). Pilate's quasi-philosophical response, "What is truth?" misses the point. Listeners may smile.

Scene three (18:38-40) has Pilate declare that he hadn't found any reason to charge Jesus, important for the drama, but especially for future generations and anyone linked to the state to hear, namely that Jesus and the Jesus movement in their midst was no danger. Don't suspect them! The author then brings the old tradition about freeing a prisoner at Passover, and has the Jews reject the release of Jesus and ask instead for Barabbas, a man whose name translated means, son of the father. Did it really happen or was it an early piece of creative story telling?

This choice of a rebel looks bad for the Jews and that will be part of the intention. The claim is that it is not the Jesus movement but Jews who are the problem for Rome. This is another instance of blame shifting. If there is history behind what looks suspiciously symbolic, then it preserves an indication that Jesus was, indeed, put into the category of subversives, Barabbas being a rebel.

Scene four (19:1-3) has Pilate have Jesus beaten. Beating up prisoners and suspects occurs often in dictatorships. Whether historical or not, it would have been thinkable for John's listeners. It would also have been filled with irony, because they knew that he really was a king, their king! Mark also brings an account of the soldiers' mockery, but it comes, as one would expect, after Pilate passes judgment on Jesus. Our author's relocation of the event to the midpoint of the set of seven exchanges that he has developed serves the drama by then enabling Pilate to present Jesus as King of the Jews.

Scene five (19:4-7) follows on closely, with Pilate for a second time declaring Jesus an innocent man. The response of the chief priests and their officers cries out for crucifixion and again Pilate tells them to do it under their own judicial system, a nonsense because he would have known that it was forbidden under Roman law, so perhaps this is simply mockery. Now the author finally has them lay their serious charge, saying he called himself the Son of God. That was a title used of kings adopted to rule as God's vice regents, such as we see in Psalm 2:7, but here much more is meant, namely what the author has been saying throughout about Jesus.

Scene six (19:8-11) has Pilate awed by this claim. Mouthing one of the key motifs of the author's image of Jesus, he asks Jesus where he's from. John's listeners know the answer well, so there is dramatic irony here. Now finally the author returns to the tradition found in Mark about Jesus keeping silent, but not for long. Pressed by Pilate for his apparent rudeness in remaining quiet, Jesus replies, effectively attributing Pilate's authority to God and putting the blame squarely on the Jews as being the more guilty ones.

The final scene, scene seven (19:12–16), has Pilate again engage the Jews and again effectively declare Jesus not guilty, wanting to release him. The contrast in guilt is thus increased in John's story. The appeal to being a friend of the emperor is shameless, but enough to persuade Pilate, who sits on the judicial seat to exercise judgment. When the author has him again confront the Jews by declaring to them that Jesus is their king, they declare they have no king but the emperor, something that would have appalled Jews hearing the story, in which it depicted the depths to which they had sunk.

The author then has Pilate hand him over to them to have him crucified. This is an extraordinary move on the author's part and reads as though the Jews are the ones who will then crucify Jesus, quite contrary to what we know happened, as he must have known. Having the Jews, themselves, lead him off to be crucified would be a highly improbable sequence of events. Perhaps the author does not mean us to read it that way, but rather that Pilate handed Jesus over to them as a result of which his soldiers would have led him off to be crucified. It nevertheless loads even more guilt on the Jews and makes Pilate seem at worst just rather weak and Jesus and his followers then and later as in no way any threat to the state. This is a sad retelling.

Amid it, the author, at the moment of Pilate's declaration, gives the time as midday on the Day of Preparation, the time after which the lambs to be consumed in the Passover meal would be butchered. Jesus too was led as a lamb to slaughter. Such imagery will play a role in what follows.

Dealing with the author's reworking of Jesus' trial before Pilate, we face a number of challenges. Historically, the likely reality is still visible: the Roman administration was bent on executing dissent and subversion and Jesus fell into that category. Callous suppression of dissent is characteristic of oppressive regimes and is designed to convey a clear message: Don't mess with power! Don't question the order, which resists change!

The author's creative elaboration of the exchange between Jesus and Pilate and Pilate and the Jews runs an agenda that shifts the blame for Jesus' death from Pilate, and more especially from Rome, to the Jewish authorities and by implication to the Jews more broadly. Pilate is still guilty for letting it happen, but that guilt is about not being a good Roman governor, who should never have let it happen. This framing of the Jews almost certainly reflects the concerns of the author and his faith communities to assure Roman authorities that they mean no harm and that the problem people are the Jews who have not joined them. Truth and love are the casualties in such reconstruction.

Reflection: History and bias meet us here: Does it matter?

Execution and Entombment (John 19:16–42)

Listening to John

19:16 So they took Jesus **17** and, carrying his own cross, he went out to the place called the Place of the Skull, called in Hebrew Golgotha, **18** where they crucified him and two others with him on either side and Jesus in the middle. **19** Pilate wrote the charge out and attached it to the cross. It read, "Jesus of Nazareth, the King of the Jews." **20** Many of the Jews therefore read the charge, because the location where Jesus was crucified was close to the city. It was written in Hebrew, Latin, and Greek. **21** So the chief priests of the Jews said to Pilate, "Don't write, "the King of the Jews," but "He said, 'I am the King of the Jews.'"

22 Pilate replied, "What I have written, I have written."

23 When they crucified Jesus, the soldiers removed his clothes and divided them into four portions and each soldier got a portion, and they removed his tunic. But the tunic was seamless, woven in one piece from top to bottom. **24** So they said to one another. "Let's not tear it but toss up for who might get it." This was so that the Scripture might be fulfilled, "They divided my garments among them and cast lots for my clothing." That's what the soldiers did.

25 Jesus' mother and his aunt, Mary daughter of Clopas, and Mary Magdalene were standing near the cross. **26** Seeing his mother and the disciple he was fond of standing alongside her, Jesus said to his mother, "Woman, look, your son." **27** Then he said to the disciple, "Look, your mother." And from that time on, the disciple took her to be with his family.

28 After this, when Jesus realized that it was all over, he said, "I'm thirsty." That was so that Scripture might be fulfilled. **29** Now there was a vessel full of sour wine sitting there. So filling a sponge with the wine and attaching it to a branch, they raised it up to his mouth. **30** When Jesus tasted the wine he said, "It's over." And bowing his head, he breathed his last breath.

31 Now, since it was the day of Preparation, and so that the bodies wouldn't stay hanging on the cross on the Sabbath—for that was an important Sabbath—the Jews asked Pilate to have their legs broken and have them taken away. **32** So the soldiers came and broke the legs of the first one and also the other one crucified along with him; **33** but coming to Jesus, when they saw he had already died, didn't break his legs. **34** Instead, one of the soldiers stabbed him in the side with his spear and immediately out came blood and water. **35** And the one who saw this has testified that it was so, and his testimony is reliable, and he knows that he's telling the truth, so that you really can believe it. **36** For this happened that the Scripture might be fulfilled, "His bones will not be broken" **37** and again the other Scripture which says, "They shall look at the one whom they stabbed."

38 After this, Joseph from Arimathea, a secret disciple of Jesus for fear of the Jews, asked Pilate if he might take Jesus' body, and Pilate permitted him to do so. So he came and took his body. **39** Nicodemus, the one who approached him first at night, came bringing a mixture of myrrh and aloes, around a hundred pounds in weight. **40** So they took Jesus' body and wrapped it in cloth with the spices, as was the custom for Jews for burials. **41** Now in that place where he was crucified there was a garden and, in the garden, a new tomb, where no one had yet been laid. **42** And there, because it was the day of Preparation of the Jews and the tomb was nearby, they put Jesus.

Thinking About John

The author's account of Jesus' crucifixion draws heavily on the tradition we know from Mark. There are some differences. If he knew it, he omits the reference to Simon of Cyrene being made to carry the cross—perhaps to emphasize Jesus' independence? Like Mark, the author names the location as Golgotha and gives the name's meaning, which fits the execution to come, the place of the skull, perhaps originally referring to its contours. Similarly, he passes on traditional detail about Jesus being crucified between two others, but without reference to their crimes. They, like Barabbas, were rebels, so belonged to the broad category of subversives, which in Pilate's assessment would have also fitted Jesus.

Our author goes beyond Mark and the other Gospels in having the charge against Jesus spelled out in three languages and adds another exchange with the Jews about its appropriateness. The upshot is that Pilate makes another declaration, "What I have written, I have written," probably intended by the author to be heard as another declaration of its truth.

Mark's narrative is informed by use of Psalm 22. Mark describes the dividing up of Jesus' garments citing Psalm 22:19: "They divide my clothes among themselves, and for my clothing they cast lots." (22:19). Whereas the other Gospels read it as describing a single event, using typical parallelism characteristic of Hebrew poetry, our author, who also cites it, delineates two events. The first is the dividing up of the clothes. The second is tossing up over what he describes as the outer garment, woven from top to bottom, hardly something to cut up! Very likely this is symbolic of the unity the author has Jesus pray for among his disciples and their successors in 17:20–21.

The second allusion to Psalm 22 in Mark is to 22:7–8, "All who see me mock at me; they make mouths at me, they shake their heads; 'Commit your cause to the Lord; let him deliver—let him rescue the one in whom he delights!'" (Mark 15:29–32). If he knew it, our author omits it, probably because one of the three mockeries related to the destroying and rebuilding of the temple, a motif our author removed from Jesus' last days, relocating it to three years earlier in chapter 2.

The author also omits Psalm 22:1, "My God, my God, why have you forsaken me" (Mark 15:34), which Matthew also preserves (27:46), but Luke already omits. It is no surprise, then, that the author of the Fourth Gospel also omits it. Nothing should suggest that God's Son, Jesus, ever felt abandoned by his Father.

The author follows the reference to dividing garments and the symbolism of the outer garment made of a single wove with an account without parallel in the other Gospels. The author begins with the tradition about the women remaining in proximity to the cross. John names them as Jesus' mother, her sister, Mary daughter of Clopas, and Mary Magdalene. Women were there, but Mark has a different list: Mary Magdalene, Mary mother of the younger James and of Joseph, and Salome. Women were there even if the lists vary. It is not insignificant that the one name in common is Mary Magdalene, who will feature in John's resurrection account.

He then has Jesus address his mother and the disciple of whom he was fond, asking him to take her into his care. If, as is likely, this disciple carries a symbolic meaning in the author's work, we might see this as an implicit claim on the part of the author (and perhaps his community) to be the true keepers of the heritage of Jesus. As noted in our discussion of Jesus' way of addressing his mother in 2:4, "Woman," so here "Woman, look, your son" is an acceptable form of address, not disrespectful or distancing and is found also elsewhere as an accepted manner of address (4:21; 20:13, 15).

John's account moves on to report Jesus' death. There is nothing here about darkness covering the land for three hours (a typically Markan play on three-ness, having Jesus crucified at the third hour, die at the sixth, and on a metaphorically dark day) (Mark 15:25, 33), let alone a torn temple curtain at Jesus' death, as in Mark (15:38; Matt 27:51), or an earthquake as in Matthew (27:51–53), symbolic elaborations. Nor have we a gentile centurion acclaiming Jesus to be Son of God, as in Mark and Matthew, and as innocent as in Luke (Mark 15:39; Matt 27:54; Luke 23:47).

Instead, in an apparent allusion to Psalm 69 ("for my thirst they gave me vinegar to drink," 69:21), the author has Jesus say he was thirsty. Mark has him offered wine mixed with myrrh apparently just before he was crucified, and again just before he died, when he cried out, "My God, my God, why have you forsaken me?" (Mark 15:23, 33). Mark tells us that, since Jesus used the Hebrew, "Eloi, Eloi," people misheard it as a cry for Elijah and again offered him wine which he rejected (Mark 15:33–36).

Our author, as we noted, does not have Jesus cry out in forsakenness using Psalm 22:1, and so has no reference to Elijah, but does have the reference to being thirsty and the offer of wine, which Jesus takes and then dies (19:28–30). His final words have been the subject of much speculation. I have chosen the simple meaning. "It's over," literally "It is finished" (19:30). The author had used the same words to introduce this final scene, "After this when Jesus realized that it was all over," or literally, "After this when Jesus realized that everything was now finished" (19:28).

The author has Jesus speak in similar terms earlier in his account. "My food is to do the will of the one who sent me and to finish his work" (4:34) and "And I have glorified you on earth, having finished the work you entrusted to me to do" (17:4). The work he has to finish was to do what he had come to do, as, for instance, John 17 explains. He has made known God's name to his chosen, told them what God has told him, fulfilled the role of an envoy, sent on God's behalf. If "finish" is to be taken literally here and not to simply mean, "It's all over," then that would be what is meant here.

Some do, however, read other meanings into "It is finished," such as his act of atonement, but that seems unlikely.

Equally open to dispute is what the author then describes as happening, "And bowing his head he breathed his last breath" or literally "he gave up his spirit." Does the author intend that we should see in this a reference to Jesus' giving the Holy Spirit back to God or giving it to his disciples? Some read it this way. This is not impossible but is very unlikely, since the author will have Jesus give the Spirit on the night of resurrection day (20:22). It is best to read simply as another way of saying: he died.

The author then brings a scene, not found in the other Gospels, and that may well have been a creative addition, the stabbing of Jesus' body resulting in blood and water coming out (19:31-37). The context makes sense: the Jews did not want the bodies to hang there during the Sabbath, not least because as the Sabbath was also the Day of Passover in John, it was a special Sabbath. That then prompts Pilate to have the soldiers take them down, breaking their legs to ensure they died.

So much reads as matter of fact, but then we have the detail that they notice that Jesus was dead already and so only stab him through his middle just in case. That would make sense. It is, at another level, an instance of fulfillment of Scripture. Thus, two prophecies can be declared fulfilled. "His bones will not be broken," probably citing Psalm 34:21 and, "They shall look at the one they speared" from Zechariah 12:10. The author may well intend that his listeners make another connection, namely with the requirement that Passover lambs should not have broken bones, thus alluding to Jesus as the Passover lamb. Seeing him as such might be why the author has him die at the time when the lambs would have been slaughtered. In 1:29, 35, the author had John the Baptist acclaim Jesus the lamb of God come to take away the world's sin. This may well be in mind here.

The author clearly had another important reason for this episode. It enabled him to report that someone really did see—he emphasizes!—that after Jesus was stabbed, blood and water came out of his body. It would certainly look like that, if you stabbed someone in their middle through their side, but it clearly mattered to point this out. Why? Very probably because it proved Jesus was really human and his body was not simply a disguise. We suspect that this is so, because in 1 John (and also reflected in 2 John) we have reference to a split in the community, apparently in part on the basis that some were claiming that Jesus only appeared to be human (1 John 2:18-19; 4:2-3; 2 John 7). Hence the author of 1 John's insistence:

he really was human: we saw him, touched him, and to deny he came in the flesh is to deny the faith (1 John 1:1).

Again, there has been speculation that the author was perhaps intending more, such as seeing in blood and water a reference to the Eucharist and baptism or the Eucharist and the Spirit. We are on more secure grounds in seeing in the reference to blood and water a claim that this shows Jesus was really human.

Joseph of Arimathea's role in retrieving the body of Jesus is noted also in the other Gospels. Earlier the author wrote critically about followers of Jesus who kept their allegiance secret (12:42–43) but does not do so here in 19:38. Luke even depicts Joseph as sharing the hope for the kingdom (23:51). Our author adds the reference to Nicodemus, who had approached Jesus with an inadequate faith (3:1-5) that was exposed as incompetent, but who had also cautioned fellow Council members about giving Jesus true justice (7:50-52).

It is very clear that Gospel writers were not happy simply to pass on the basic facts of what happened, however much they did or did not know, but were also keen to retell the story in ways that brought out its significance. Either Mark or someone before Mark used the imagery of Psalm 22 to fill in the gaps. Mark then plays with three-ness and with atmosphere in the sense of having the day turn dark, as indeed it did metaphorically. Having a gentile confess what God had declared at Jesus' baptism and transfiguration was a way of celebrating the gentile mission. Luke's having one of the rebels repent and believe was part of his elaboration.

John's elaborations appear to relate especially to the division that we suspect he was fearing in his faith communities, in danger of tearing unity apart. This unity was to be upheld by staying with the witness to Jesus he represented as one with Jesus' favorite disciple and his mother, and faithful to the memory of Jesus as truly the Word made flesh.

Behind all the elaborations is the stark memory of a shameful crucifixion and of Jesus as dispensed with because he fell into the category of people who subverted the peace by challenging Rome's order, whether by sword or by word. Faithful to fulfilling that challenge and affirming hope of change, he met that end, or as our author would put it, he was God's faithful envoy offering love and change to the end and so his death was a revelation of their sin and his and God's love.

Reflection: Imagine you are one of the author's first listeners: What would you take from this account?

Easter and Pentecost All in One (John 20:1–31)

Listening to John

20:1 On the first day of the week Mary Magdalene came very early while it was still dark to the tomb and saw that the rock had been removed from in front of the tomb. **2** So she ran and approached Simon Peter and the other disciple Jesus was fond of and told them, "They've taken the Lord out of the tomb, and we've no idea where they've put him." **3** So Peter and the other disciple set off and came to the tomb. **4** The two of them ran together, but the other disciple ran faster than Peter and was the first to get to the tomb. **5** And stooping down, he saw the clothes lying there, but didn't go in. **6** Simon Peter, following after him, also came and went into the tomb and saw the clothes lying there, **7** together with the wrapping that had been around his head. It was not lying with the clothes but folded up in a place on its own. **8** Then the other disciple, the one who had arrived first at the tomb, also went inside and saw and believed, for they didn't yet know the Scripture that he must rise from the dead. **10** So the disciples returned again to the others.

11 Now Mary was standing outside near the tomb weeping. As she was crying, she stooped to look inside the tomb **12** and saw two angels dressed in white sitting there, one at the head and one at the feet where Jesus' body had been. **13** And they asked her, "Woman, why are you crying?"

She told them, "Because they've taken my Lord away, and I've no idea where they've put him." **14** Having spoken these words, she turned around and saw Jesus standing there but didn't recognize that it was Jesus.

15 Jesus said to her, "Woman, why are you weeping? Who are you looking for?"

She, thinking it was the gardener, told him, "Sir, if you took him away, tell me where you put him, and I'll get him."

16 Jesus said to her, "Mary."

Turning round, she said to him in Hebrew, "Rabbouni," which means "Teacher."

[17] Jesus told her, "Don't hold onto me, because I haven't returned to my Father yet, but go to my brothers and tell them, 'I'm going back up to my Father and your Father, to my God and your God.'"

[18] Mary Magdalene went to the disciples and announced to them, "I've seen the Lord," and told them what he had told her.

[19] In the evening on that day, the first day of the week, when the doors were locked where the disciples were for fear of the Jews, Jesus came and stood among them and said to them, "Peace be with you." [20] And having said this, he showed them his hands and his side. The disciples were overjoyed to see the Lord. [21] So he said to them, again, "Peace be with you. As my Father sent me, so I'm sending you." [22] And having said this, he breathed on and them and said, "Receive the Holy Spirit. [23] If you forgive the sins of anyone, they'll be forgiven, and if you stay holding them guilty, they'll be considered guilty."

[24] Thomas, one of the twelve, called the Twin, wasn't there with them when Jesus came. [25] So the other disciples began to tell him, "We've seen the Lord!"

He said to them, "Unless I see the nail mark in his hands and can put my finger into the nail mark and put my hand into his side I am not going to believe."

[26] Now eight days later his disciples were again inside, and Thomas was there, too, and Jesus arrived through the closed doors and stood in the middle of them and said, "Peace be with you." [27] Then he said to Thomas, "Put your finger here and look at my hands and take your hand and put it in my side; don't disbelieve, be a believer."

[28] In response Thomas said, "My Lord and my God!"

[29] Jesus said to him, "You've seen and believed; happy are those who come to believe without seeing."

[30] Now Jesus did many other miracles in the presence of his disciples, which are not written in this book, [31] but these are written so that you may believe that Jesus is the Messiah, the Son of God, and that believing you might have life in his name.

Thinking About John

John's account of Jesus' resurrection begins with Mary Magdalene. Mark has her accompanied by two others who had been with her at the site of Jesus' execution. In Mark's story the women do not encounter the risen Jesus but receive instruction from a young man dressed in white that they are to tell the disciples that Jesus would meet Peter and the others in Galilee (16:7). However, they didn't say anything to anyone because they were scared (16:8).

Matthew has Mary plus one other; but, as in John's Gospel, they do encounter Jesus. He meets them when they are on their way to the disciples. He then gives them the instructions directly about his going to meet the disciples in Galilee (28:9-10). Matthew adds an earthquake to his story and has an angel rolling the rock away and then sitting on it (28:2). Luke follows Mark in having the women who had followed Jesus from Galilee, including Mary Magdalene, come to the tomb (24:1), but in his version, they are met by two men in shiny clothes (24:4). They tell them Jesus is alive, and so they run off to tell the disciples. Peter then runs to the tomb and looks in and sees Jesus' clothes lying there (24:12).

Clearly, whatever was the original story, it has undergone legendary embellishments. Even Mark's account, the earliest, has a quaint figure telling the women what happened, but, even more strangely, implies that the story of the women must have come up after the first encounter with the risen Jesus in Galilee. For they had said nothing and must have reported their experience only after the promised encounter in Galilee. Perhaps this is closer to what actually happened, but some would see the entire story about the women and the tomb as legendary.

There is therefore considerable complexity and diversity already in the other Gospels when they tell this story. It should not surprise us to find even more in the account given by the author of John's Gospel, whose creativity in retelling traditional stories we have regularly encountered. It has just Mary Magdalene on the scene. This works best for the very personal story of her encounter with Jesus. Is this his adaptation or was it originally only Mary who came to the tomb? We may never know. The rock's removal and the absence of the corpse made sense of the fear that someone had removed it.

Some details appear to reflect the author's typical creativity. He opts to follow a version reflected in Luke that has Peter run to the tomb, but then appears to have added the disciple of whom Jesus was fond into the narrative, whom he uses elsewhere as a kind of guarantor for his version of the Gospel. He outruns Peter. Why mention this? Probably because it formed part of his agenda to show respect for Peter and his traditional leadership, on the one hand, but to claim this disciple as the guarantor for his account and its superiority. He was first there and first to see and first to believe, even though Peter was the first to enter. It seems a likely embellishment, but one can never be sure.

Having Jesus' clothes in one pile but the wrappings that had been around his head folded up on their own, a detail absent from the other versions of story, is another likely addition of the author. It tells the listener that Jesus himself must have done it. The author's comment that neither Peter nor the other disciple knew the Scripture according to which Jesus was to rise from the dead explains their surprise and highlights that that other disciple was the first of the disciples to believe, crossing the finishing line ahead of Peter.

Following Mark's story, we would assume that, as the mysterious young man told the women, Jesus would appear to Peter and the disciples in Galilee as promised (16:7). This implies that Peter was the first to encounter the risen Jesus, and this appears to be assumed also elsewhere, such as by Luke when he has the disciples tell those who had arrived from the Emmaus Road: "The Lord has risen indeed, and he has appeared to Simon!' (24:34). Paul, too, our earliest witness, when reporting the tradition he had passed on to him about Jesus, notes that Peter was the first to see him as risen: "he was raised on the third day in accordance with the scriptures, and that he appeared to Cephas [Peter], then to the twelve" (1 Cor 15:4–5). The author of John's Gospel, instead, has his favorite disciple as the first to believe, ahead of Peter, but also has Mary Magdalene as the first to encounter Jesus, similar to Matthew, who has Jesus encounter the women at the tomb.

A new dramatic episode follows after Peter and the other disciple return, presumably, to the rest of the disciples, literally, "to them" (20:10). Mary plucks up courage and enters the tomb and sees two angels who ask her why she is weeping, and they listen to her concern. The drama heightens. She turns and sees Jesus. Mistaken for the gardener and asked where he might have taken the corpse, Jesus addresses Mary by name, and she hails her teacher. It is a wonderful story the author is telling.

The author has indeed portrayed Jesus as a teacher, an envoy sent to communicate God's offer of life and so, consistent with his particular way of framing Jesus' life, he has Jesus tell her not to hold onto him, at a human level, but to let him go because he needed to return to his Father. This might recall for John's listeners what he had Jesus explain to his disciples in his farewell words to them, namely about his returning to the Father and how he would then send the Spirit.

According to John's account, Mary met him while he was still on his way to the Father, but by evening he obviously had returned and so could give the Spirit (20:19–23). Having the doors locked was not just for fear of the Jews. In the narrative it was also to highlight the new kind of existence that Jesus had assumed. Following much Jewish belief at the time, resurrection entailed transforming the physical corpse into a spiritual body which had the capacity to appear and disappear, so it could materialize in closed off contexts. The author appears at this point to be adapting Luke's account of Jesus' appearance (24:36–49), which includes the greeting of peace, the showing of the marks of crucifixion on his body, and the commissioning of the disciples.

The greeting of "Peace" can mean little more than "hello," but will, at least emotionally, be understood to mean much more, and understandably the disciples are joyous and the author depicts Jesus showing his wounds (including the stab wound, unique to his account).

There is a clear commissioning of the disciples, using the envoy model which had shaped the author's depiction of Jesus and his significance, the golden thread running through the Gospel. He was sent from God and came from above. They are now sent by Jesus. The implication is that their task is the same. They are to be envoys of God, offering God's invitation to life. It is fitting then, that he goes on to speak of the Spirit, which would inspire and enable them to fulfill this task. This had been the promise he made to the disciples in his farewell words to them (14:16–17).

The author links Jesus' gift of the Spirit implicitly to the creation story, according to which God made a clay model of a human, breathed on it, and it came to life (Gen 2:7). This is suggestive of a new beginning. Breath, wind, spirit are all the same word in Greek and Hebrew, so playful associations and ambiguities could enrich meaning and the author, as we have observed, is very adept at using words with multiple meaning to great effect. The author relates the gift of the Spirit not just to the disciples' commission but also to their need to handle discipline issues in their community, perhaps another indication of the author's concerns about unity and division (20:23).

The Thomas episode (22:24–29) has had much appeal in acknowledging the validity of doubt, but the author has Jesus offer the proofs of nail marks and the stab wound and affirms Thomas' response, "My Lord and my God!" but tempers it with the declaration that those will be more blessed who don't need such proof but simply believe.

The last two verses read as though we have reached the end of the Gospel and perhaps that was once the case, but now the author has added a final chapter. The focus appears to be on the miracles, so many of them, but the author's emphasis throughout has been on the deeper meaning they convey, often symbolically, but also literally that Jesus was indeed God's Son who came in the flesh. His aim, however, was to bring people to faith and keep people in the faith that they might have life.

This first set of resurrection stories have their own distinctive traits which doubtless go back to the author's creativity, but behind them is the firm faith that God did indeed raise Jesus from the dead. It differs from Mark, who has women find the tomb empty and a young man point them to Peter's encounter with Jesus in Galilee, matching what we find in Paul and a tradition in Luke. It is closer in that sense to Matthew who has Jesus encounter the women, but who also points to Galilee and reports the disciples' commissioning on a proverbial mountain top.

Luke put the events within a symbolic framework, having Jesus make such appearances for forty days, then ascend and then on the fiftieth day, the literal meaning of word "Pentecost," have the Spirit descend. It was fitting that it occur on this day which celebrated harvest and also the giving the Law on Sinai. What John depicts as happening all on Easter Day, Luke spreads over fifty days. Luke's structure has shaped the church year, but clearly Luke was aware that reality was a little different, especially because he later has the risen Jesus appearing to Paul on the road to Damascus long after the forty days and the day of Pentecost.

Behind all these stories, diverse as they are and so creatively embellished, is the common thread that saw Rome's no to Jesus met by God's yes, and Jesus vindicated by resurrection. The author makes very clear that Jesus' resurrection was not the end of the story. The commissioning and the gift of the Spirit meant the offer of life in relationship with God, eternal life, an offer that must go on. That task now falls to the disciples and their successors who now need to share that love effectively with one another and make it known to the world. That too would have its complications, so the author has yet more to say.

Reflection: Most Jews already believed in life after death and resurrection, so what is the significance of Jesus' resurrection behind the stories and according to the Fourth Gospel?

Where to from Here? (John 21:1–25)

Listening to John

21:1 After this Jesus showed himself again to his disciples by Lake Tiberias. This is how he did it. **2** Simon Peter and Thomas called the Twin and Nathanael from Cana of Galilee and the sons of Zebedee and two other disciples were all together.

3 Simon Peter said to them, "I'm going fishing."

They said, "We're coming, too."

They set off and got into a boat and that night they caught nothing. **4** Early next morning Jesus was standing on the shore. The disciples, however, didn't recognize it was Jesus. **5** Jesus said to them, "You guys, have you caught any fish?"

They answered, "Nope."

6 Then he said to them, "Throw your net out on the starboard side of the boat, and you'll get some." So they threw their net and found they weren't able to haul it in because it was full of fish.

7 The disciple Jesus was fond of said to Peter, "It's the Lord."

So when Simon Peter heard it was the Lord, he tucked his coat around his waist, because he hadn't had any clothes on, and dived into the lake, **8** while the other disciples came in the boat. For they were not far from land, just around 200 cubits away (approximately 100 yards or meters) and came dragging the net full of fish with them.

9 When they got out onto dry land, they saw a fire set up there and some fish and bread. **10** Jesus said to them, "Bring some of the fish you've just now caught."

11 So Simon Peter went on board and dragged the net to land full of big fish, 153 of them, so many but still the net was not torn.

12 Jesus told them, "Come and eat."

None of the disciples dared to quiz him asking, "Who are you?" because they recognized it was the Lord.

¹³ Jesus came and took the bread and distributed it among them and similarly the fish. ¹⁴ This was now the third time Jesus showed himself to his disciples after he was raised from the dead.

¹⁵ When they had eaten, Jesus said to Simon Peter, "Simon son of John, do you love me more than these?"

He said to him, "Yes, Lord, you know that I love you."

Jesus told him, "Feed my lambs."

¹⁶ A second time he said to him again, "Simon son of John, do you love me?"

He responded, "Yes, Lord, you know that I love you."

Jesus told him, "Look after my sheep."

¹⁷ He said to him a third time, "Simon, son of John, do you love me?"

Peter was upset that he asked him a third time, "Do you love me?" and so replied, "Lord, you know everything; you know that I love you."

Jesus told him, "Feed my sheep. ¹⁸ Truly, truly, I tell you, when you were a younger man, you dressed yourself up and went off travelling wherever you wanted, but when you're an old man, you will stretch out your hands and someone else will dress you up and carry you where you won't want to go." ¹⁹ He said this to indicate by what kind of death he was going to glorify God, and having said this, he told him, "Follow me!"

²⁰ So Peter, turned round and saw the disciple whom Jesus was fond of following behind. He was the one who had rested close to Jesus' chest during their last meal, and had asked, "Lord, who is it that's going to betray you?"

²¹ So Peter seeing him said to Jesus, "Lord, what about him?"

²² Jesus told him, "If I want him to stay around until I return, what's that to you? So you just follow me!"

²³ This comment circulated among the brothers, namely that that disciple wouldn't die. But Jesus didn't say he wouldn't die, but rather, "If I decide that he stay around till I come."

²⁴ This is the disciple who is testifying to these things and who has written them up, and we know that his testimony is reliable. ²⁵ There are many other things which Jesus did. I reckon that if they were all written down, the world would not have enough room for the books that would be written.

THE END AND THE BEGINNING

Thinking About John

After thinking at the end of John 20 that we might have reached the end of John's Gospel, we find the author beginning again. This time we are in Galilee. Mark's Easter story has the angels tell the women to inform Peter that Jesus would appear to them in Galilee (16:7), and the reference to Peter's encounter with Jesus as where it all began for the disciples meets us already in Paul (1 Cor 15:4) and also in Luke (24:34), as we have noted above. Nowhere, however, do we have an account of that encounter with Peter except perhaps here, although it does not read as a first encounter and is, according to the author, the third encounter thus far (21:14).

This first story in John 21 raises a number of questions. One relates to its original setting. Luke brings the story of men returning from fishing, not having caught anything, and then at Jesus' suggestion making a big catch (5:1–11). In Luke's story, Jesus got into Peter's boat and told him go out further and try again, with the result that they netted such a huge catch of fish that their nets were in danger of breaking and so had to call for help from their colleagues, James and John, sons of Zebedee. That was Luke's version of what in Mark had been more simply about Jesus walking along the shore, seeing them, and challenging them to follow him (1:16–20).

Clearly a story was in circulation that connected the miraculous catch of fish with Peter and his commission, and we have two versions of it. Was it originally about Peter encountering the risen Jesus, as in John, or about his original call to become a disciple? The challenge, "Follow me!," twice expressed in John's account, seems to fit his initial calling better. We may never know the story's origin, whether Luke or John was right.

Both stories reflect the image that Mark has Jesus use when he tells Peter, "Follow me, and I will have you fish for people!" Mission, winning others to become followers of Jesus, was the new task. John's reference to there being 153 fish is doubtless symbolic, but precisely how is uncertain. Was it the belief that there were 153 different kinds of fish in their world?

Our author typically develops the story in his own way and with his own concerns. Once again, his hero, the unnamed disciple described as the one whom Jesus was especially fond of, comes first in recognizing Jesus. The list of names of those who had joined Peter in going fishing includes the sons of Zebedee (James and John, though not named here) as in Luke's story, but also Thomas, Nathanael, and two others. Was the favored disciple one of the others or, as tradition came to believe, John, son of Zebedee? The author clearly had no interest in giving us his name.

John's story is full of drama. Peter dives into the lake and swims ashore. An element not in Luke's story is the lakeside fire that Jesus had laid, with already some fish and bread. Listeners to the story would very likely have seen in this an allusion to the Eucharist and to the feeding of the five thousand. He has them bring some of their fish. It is slightly awkward that the author has the disciples hesitate to ask Jesus who he was, given that they already knew. Perhaps the author knew of Luke's story, according to which the risen Jesus made himself known to his disciples in the breaking of the bread (24:35). It is likely that for the author and his listeners, meeting to celebrate Holy Communion was a central element of their faith and of their awareness of Jesus' presence.

There follows the famous interchange between Jesus and Peter in which Jesus asks Peter three times whether he loves him and, on receiving an affirmative answer, tells him to feed his sheep. There is some variation in the words Jesus used; sheep and lambs; and in the word for love, but these are insignificant. The focus is on the commission to leadership of future disciples, portrayed as sheep, an image the author had already used to good effect in John 10.

The threefold exchange clearly echoes Peter's threefold denial of Jesus and so indicates his rehabilitation. There is forgiveness and grace for a new beginning. The assumption is that Peter has faced up to what he has done, not that Jesus pretended it had not occurred or swept it under the carpet, as has sadly sometimes happened where leaders have failed. Perhaps asking three times indicates awareness of Peter's fallibility. All leaders are fallible.

Clearly, for all his emphasis on his favorite disciple, the author acknowledged Peter's special leadership position. Ultimately that will have had to do with Peter's role in being the first to encounter the risen Jesus, according to early tradition, and his therefore being the rock, the foundation, on which the future church would rest, as Matthew's tradition puts it (16:18). The author alludes to Peter's death, which legend later portrayed as an upside-down crucifixion. That death occurred in the time of Nero, around 64 CE.

The exchange that follows has Peter ask about the disciple whom the author of this gospel has been depicting as superior to Peter, at least in insight. The author appears to be addressing a real issue, namely that some had come to believe that this disciple would still be alive when Jesus returned. By the author's time, Jesus had not returned, and the disciple had died, so an explanation was needed, which the author supplies.

This correction is also interesting in the light of what then follows, where the author claims that same disciple as the authority for his Gospel, which he also implicitly claims is superior to previous Gospels. The closing statement could be read as though the author is claiming to be that disciple, but that can hardly be so. Rather, the loved disciple is the one to whom the author appeals as the reliable basis for his creative portrait of Jesus. This person may well have been one of Jesus' first disciples, who had helped found and shape the communities of faith in which our author writes. It was not uncommon to make such claims to authorship and authority by identifying a significant leader of the past and writing in their name. Something similar is occurring when people wrote letters in Paul's name.

There's more to tell. That was how what was probably the author's earlier version of his work ended in the closing words of chapter 20, and here, at the end of John 21, the message is the same. This final chapter brings us again into connection with some of the concerns that will have driven the author to write. Confident that what he presents is the best so far of the Gospels, for which he claims insider information through the figure of the loved disciple, the author gently tiptoes around the issues of relations with the wider church. He never puts Peter and the churches he represents down. All belong, even if he claims greater wisdom.

Peter's is a story of grace. Mission is about winning followers, new disciples of Jesus, who would embrace his message as conveyed in the author's Gospel, namely as the one who came from God offering life on God's behalf. The focus was not a place nor a future event in time, but a person, namely the person of God. The author reshaped his heritage of Jesus stories to focus on a single theme: the offer of life, depicted now in terms that would have universal appeal: water, bread, light, life. That is the golden thread running through his Gospel. To do so, he retold the story to depict Jesus as the Word, God's Word, in that sense, God, but as God's Son. He came, sent by the Father as God's envoy, to offer God's gift of life in relation with himself, and to return and have the Spirit sent to keep the offer going. That offer could now reach out beyond Jesus' setting to the world.

That community needed to hold together, to feed itself on the word of the Gospel and through the bread and wine representing him and his presence, and to be a community of mutual love such that the world would observe and take note. That did not mean ignoring difference and not striving for excellence, but it did mean affirming of leadership and not ignoring human fallibility. Would this vision last? The Epistle of 1 John suggests that for some it did not.

Reflection: Leadership matters, and the author addresses it: What might this chapter say for our understanding of leadership?

Concluding Reflection

THE GOSPEL ACCORDING TO John is one of the treasures of the early Christian movement. Very early people began to speak of it as the "spiritual Gospel" in contrast to the other three. In doing so they were recognizing its different character and emphases. The author has taken traditions such as we find them in the other Gospels and integrated them within a narrative that develops them to be bearers of a consistent message. That message, which runs like a golden thread through the Gospel, is about Jesus offering God's gift of life, eternal life, understood less in terms of being everlasting and more in terms of the quality of sharing God's life now and in the future.

The author brings this offer of life in a manner that echoes what Jewish authors had claimed of the Law, Torah, as the expression of God's Word and Wisdom. To live by Torah was to live in oneness with God, keeping the commandments and walking in God's ways. God's Word and Wisdom was life, met the deep human spiritual thirst and hunger, and was a guide and light along the way, and as the truth was indeed the way to life. This rich spiritual tradition then informed the author's redrawn portrait of Jesus, seen also as God's gift, the climax of God's dealing with Israel and indeed the world. That portrait now presents Jesus as the bearer of the water of life, the bread of life, to meet deep spiritual hunger and thirst and as the one who brings light into darkness and becomes the way and the truth embodied in a human being.

The author adapts the model of the envoy to give expression to the faith that saw Jesus as the new embodiment and incarnation of God's Wisdom and Word. Indeed, Jesus was the Word, who like Wisdom was God's child, now pictured as the Son sent by the Father to offer the invitation to life in oneness with God. His message was not information but invitation, his claim was to be the bearer of that love offered to all and to sustain that offering even in the face of rejection and ultimately of death. His death, then, like his life, was an offering of life, also seen as like a sacrifice for sins, and as an act of judgment that exposed to the world both its sin and Jesus' goodness, and so was the means to disempower the powers of evil.

Playing, as it were, a single melody across many instruments, the author brings traditions into harmony around a single theme: the offer of life. Sometimes the claims must assert themselves against those whom the author depicts as misreading the message, as though Jesus was claiming to be a god beside God. Throughout the Gospel the envoy model asserts and reasserts not an equality with God but Jesus' identity as the Son promoting not himself but God, as God's agent and envoy to offer God's life. Claims to be the bread, the light, the life, the way, and truth were never anything other than claims to mirror or reflect and embody God's life. God remains God, and eternal life is to share God's life.

The reconfiguring of the meaning of Jesus so that the focus fell on God's offer of a relationship of life and love produced, therefore, a story that addressed universal human values and human needs. This was a shift from putting the focus on events, such as the coming of the kingdom of God or the fulfillment of Israel's hopes for a messianic kingdom. Such hopes, which do find expression in the Gospel, are now incorporated within its wider universal appeal and its depiction of the gospel as an offer of life in oneness with God the creator. In that sense it brings the Christian message close to what Jews and fellow Jews had acclaimed of God, Law and Word.

While seemingly making claims that appeared far from those Jewish claims, the radical simplification, which in one sense reduced the message to a basic offer of life with God and redrew the image of Jesus to embody God's offer of love, has produced a Gospel that puts God at the center of spirituality and reflects the rich heritage of Jewish spirituality. For the effect of its elevated images of Jesus is, in that sense, to reconfigure him to be primarily a window and mirror through or in which to see God. The result is thus to put God at the center of spirituality, and in particular to portray an image of God whose chief interest is engaging human beings in a relationship of love, and to let such love inform not only spirituality but also what it means to be in human community.

The Gospel's appeal is therefore universal in its scope as it addresses deep human need. Much of its message comes through in terms that are defensive and exclusive, reflecting tensions that the author and his community will have experienced, and sometimes their hurt has become anger, and dangerously so. Its positive claims, however, have a truth about them that can transcend the monopoly and exclusivity it sometimes claims. It is indeed the way of love that leads to life and oneness with God, and this we can affirm wherever we see it and need not to be limited to specific cultural expression. Such light wears no labels wherever it shines, and this Gospel helps us identify it as the love of which the author has Jesus speak, whether expressed in his name and wearing a Christian label or known only as love. Transforming specific traditions to become a single witness to God's offer of love invites such openness and confronts us with its absence wherever that occurs and invites to celebrate it, also wherever it occurs.

www.ingramcontent.com/pod-product-compliance
Lightning Source LLC
Chambersburg PA
CBHW020053200426
43197CB00050B/1094